D1096940

Petzoldt Hiking, National Outdoor Leadership School photo.

Petzoldt's Teton Trails

A Hiking Guide to the Teton Range
With
Stories, History, and Personal Experiences

By:

Paul Petzoldt

Senior Advisor For

NATIONAL OUTDOOR LEADERSHIP SCHOOL

Edited by: Mel Davis

Published By

WASATCH PUBLISHERS, INC.

Salt Lake City, Utah

Paul Petzoldt, Jackson Hole News photo by Cammie Pyle.

No mountains in the world are like the Tetons. Other mountains have foothills, but the Tetons plunge straight out of the flat valley into the clouds.

Copyright: 1976
Wasatch Publishers, Inc.
4647 Idlewild Rd.
Salt Lake City, Utah 84117

ISBN o-915272-05-9

Cover: Photo by Bill Eppridge, Time-Life Picture Agency, © Time Inc.

Acknowledgements:

I wish to express my thanks and appreciation to the following people for their advice, information, and photographs:

George Hunker, National Outdoor Leadership School, Lander, Wyoming.

Tony Bevenetto, National Park Service, Washington, D.C.

Pete Hart, Teton National Park, Moose, Wyoming.

Scott Phillips, Bridger-Teton National Forest, Jackson, Wyoming.

Mike Whitfield, Targhee National Forest, Driggs, Idaho.

Wayne Jenkins, Targhee National Forest, Ashton, Idaho.

Paul Petzoldt

5

From
WHO'S WHO IN AMERICA
Petzoldt, Paul, mountaineer; b. Creston, Ia., Jan. 16, 1908; s.
Charles and Emma (Kiesow) P.; student U. Ida., 1929-30, U.
Wyo., 1931, U. Utah, 1932, U. La., 1934, 35; scholar at Deanery,
Windsor Castle, Eng., 1933; m. Patricia McGarrity, June 16,
1935; m. 2d, Dorothy Dewhurst Reed, Dec. 29, 1962. Made
ascent Grand Teton, Wyo., 1924; established profl. mountain-
eering guide service, Teton Range, 1924-55; dir. Am. Sch.
Mountaineering, Jackson Hole, Wyo., 1928-55; made double
traverse Matterhorn in one day, 1934; 1st ascent N. face, Grand
Teton, 1936; 1st winter ascent Grand Teton, 1936; discovery,
reconnaissance Abruzzi Ridge Route, K2, Karakorum Range,
Kashmire, 1938, including new altitude record for Americans;
exploration, 1st ascents Sierra Nev. de Santa Marta Range, S.
Am., 1941; numerous 1st ascents, new routes mountains Wind
River and Teton Range, 1924-64; numerous rescue attempts,
1941—; chief instr. Colo. Outward Bound Sch., 1964; organized
mountaineering sch. for youth development program Lander,
Wyo., 1963; dir. Nat. Outdoor Leadership School, Lander.
Served with 10th Mountain Div., AUS, 1943-46; ETO. Recipient
Conservation Award Dept. Interior, 1951. Mem. Kappa Sigma.
Author pamphlet. Developed mountaineering voice signals,
1924-28, sliding middle man snow climbing technique, 1925-28,
also methods rhythmatic breathing, pressure breathing, salt
and water intake, food consumption, body heat control for
endurance, prevention mountain sickness, adjustment to high
altitudes. Home: Lander WY 82520 Office: Nat. Outdoor
Leadership Sch. Lander WY 82520.

I want to go soon and live away by the pond,
where I shall hear only the wind whispering among
the reeds. . . . But my friends ask what will I
do when I get there. Will it not be employment
enough to watch the progress of the seasons?

—Henry David Thoreau

Contents

Maps:
Teton Range 45
Teton Park Center 72
Teton Park North 101
Teton Park South, Bridger-Teton Forest 110
Targhee South 125
Targhee North 139
Petzoldt Stories 11
My First Grand Teton Climb 11
The Petzoldt Carving 14
On Enjoying the Outdoors 16
About Women in the Outdoors 19
On Frozen Feet 20
A Near-Tragic Climb 22
On Giving Directions 25
On Weather and Getting Lost 26
On Losing Your Direction 28
On Getting Turned Around 29
On Poaching 30
Introduction to the Tetons 33
Trip Considerations 33
Weather 34
Time Control 34
Energy Control 35
Conserving Energy 36
Clothing 38
Camping for Conservation 42
Summer Snow Techniques 44

Grand Teton National Park .47
Hiking and Backcountry Camping 47
Seeing Wildlife in Teton Park 50
Camping Information 53
Teton National Park Trails .57
Amphitheater Lake Trail 57
Garnet Canyon Trail 65
Bradley Lake Trail 73
Taggart Lake Trail 75
Death Canyon Trail 76
Open Canyon Trail 80
Granite Canyon Trail 81
Rendezvous Mountain Trail 82
Avalanche Canyon Route 84
Hidden Falls Trail 87
Cascade Canyon Trail 88
Hanging Canyon Route 91
Paintbrush Canyon Trail 94
Leigh Canyon-Moran Canyon Route 97
Berry Creek Trail 102
Owl Creek Trail 106
Webb Canyon Trail 108
Bridger-Teton National Forest 109
Phillips Pass Trail 111
Phillips Canyon Trail 112
Targhee National Forest .114
Hiking Information 114
Coal Creek Trail 117
Taylor Mountain Trail 119
Moose Creek Trail 120
Game Creek Trail 122
Fox Creek Trail 123
Darby Creek Trail 127

South Teton Canyon Trail 130
North Teton Canyon Trail 132
Freds Mountain Trail 134
South Leigh Creek Trail 135
North Fork Leigh Creek Trail 137
South Badger Creek Trail...................140
South Bitch Creek Trail 141
North Bitch Creek Trail 144
Hominy Creek (Jackass) Trail 145
South Boone Creek Trail 146
High Adventure Trail 147

Petzoldt Camping, National Outdoor Leadership School photo by Allan M. Sicks.

Petzoldt Stories

MY FIRST GRAND TETON CLIMB

"In July 1924," wrote Billy Owen, "two young college boys, Ralph Herron of Newton, Iowa and Paul Petzoldt of Twin Falls, Idaho, hiked over the mountains to Jackson, Wyoming announcing their determination to climb the Grand Teton. I chanced to be summering at Jackson at the time and a citizen of the place whom the boys met upon their arrival here, sent them to me for information relative to the proposed ascent. I gave the boys a warm welcome and congratulated them upon their resolution. They were full of fire and enthusiasm and said they were more than happy to shake hands with one of the first men who climbed the Grand Teton. They said they were desirous of 'doing something no one else had done', so I recommended an attempt on the east side of the peak. They eagerly approved my

11

suggestion and a few days later my good friend Mr. Newell Haines drove the boys to a point on the Cottonwood about five miles from the mountain and we started them on their trip up the Teton. This was July 22, and the boys that day climbed to the timberline where they remained all night. The following day they attacked the peak on the east face and by heroic efforts, fighting their way through a blizzard which enveloped them shortly after they left camp, these two young men reached an altitude of about 13,000 feet. At this point the granite had become so slippery from sleet and snow that farther advance upward was out of the question, and with frost-bitten fingers they began their perilous descent over crags and slopes whereon a single misstep meant instant destruction. But even with all these conditions against them and the blizzard still raging they decided to try for the summit on the west side and snatch victory from the jaws of defeat. With hardly any bedding, and less food, they stuck to their task, and working their way to the west side of the peak, reached the summit at one p.m., Friday, July 25. They remained on the top three hours photographing, taking notes, and chiseling their names in the granite, and returned to Jackson the following day. This is the first recorded attempt on the east side of the Teton, but someone had evidently tried it before for the boys, at a low altitude found a can, dark and rusted and also some characters on the hard granite unmistakeably placed there by human hands."

"Actually," Petzoldt says, "When Mr. Owen and Mr. Haines let us out of the Essex that morning in front of the Grand Teton, we ran for the top. We did not camp at timberline, but rushed for the summit that same day, even though we got a late start, having driven over the wagon roads through the sagebrush from Jackson. We were benighted high on the east ridge in a howling summer blizzard. We barely got back. So desperate was our situation on the east ridge that, at one point, we had to cut steps in the ice with a pocket knife and frost-bitten fingers.

That was the night of the 22nd. On the 23rd, we luckily got back to timberline and a fire and rested and recuperated the next day. Although we were out of food, we were too proud to admit defeat and face the population of Jackson, many of whom thought we wouldn't make it and some who thought all who had claimed to have reached the top were damned liars.

Our ascent on July 25th was most difficult, because we had to traverse the mountain from the base of the east ridge around to the big saddle, a different route than that taken by the others. This route was up hundreds of feet of steep snow that we climbed with the aid of handmade alpenstocks. Upon joining the Owen route on the upper big saddle, we raced to the top. There, we found records of previous climbers. We added our names as the fourth party to reach the top.

We knew that we could not go back down the steep snow slopes we had climbed that morning, because it was easy to slip on snow that had frozen to ice in the late afternoon chill. We chose a gentler slope on the Middle Teton glacier and descended down Bradley Canyon to timberline. A huge ridge a thousand feet high separated us from our blankets in the canyon to the north at the base of the east ridge. In the last twilight, we reached the top of a ridge. As we scrambled over the lip, we were surprised by a lake in a large, flat area surrounded by trees. We called it Surprise Lake, a name that still remains.

We found our blankets sometime during the night. Our shoes were disintegrated and my feet were cut and bleeding. That night, I expressed to Ralph my determination to learn how to plan for such climbs, as I knew that we had over-rated ourselves terrifically and underestimated the mountain. We had been lucky.

The next morning, with our feet wrapped in blankets, we hobbled down from timberline to the wagon road we had left five days before. A rare tourist who had braved the road from Yellowstone, picked us up and dropped us to the main square at Jackson. Several people gathered around us, skeptical that we had been successful. Soon, Billy Owen came running across the street. He questioned us about what we had seen and then put his hand on my shoulder and said, "Folks, these boys have been to the top of the Grand Teton."

THE PETZOLDT CARVING

I was sort of the last of the old timers. Carving names or initials on trees was quite customary in the early days. After all, I think one of the great treasures of Yellowstone is the pieces cut out of trees with Colters name on it. Owen had carved his initials on top of the Grand Teton as had Rev. Spaulding and the other people there.

I think I was sort of motivated in those days to have the romantic idea of leaving my name on one of the great trees in the Tetons. I don't remember correctly now why I did it as it's been over fifty years ago.

I carved my whole last name and the date on a huge beautiful Douglas fir and to my knowledge when I went to see it again in 1974 no one had been there since I carved it in 1924. It's in a sort of a moist place in a small valley on the way up the Grand Teton. The tree must be around four and a half feet in diameter now.

It was in 1924 and I think it was on the second trip after Ralph Herron and I made the successful climb to the top. Billy Owen, who had made the first successful climb to the top of the Grand, knowing that we had just been up and knew the way, and he being somewhat older than us, hired me to lead this party up the Grand Teton.

I had scouted out a way to bring horses part way up the Grand into Bradley Canyon (now Garnet Canyon). Through various intricate routes we got the horses into this little meadow and that's where we made our camp. While we were camping there was when I carved my name on this tree. And I knew it was there for forty or fifty years. But after I started to climb the Grand Teton more and more, and had become a little bit educated in conservation, I was always somewhat ashamed of it and I didn't want to take people there and brag about it.

In 1974, on the occasion of the 50th anniversary of my ascent of the Grand Teton, we camped there on the way up. I took some of the people over to see it and there it was. It was grown over beautifully and all those letters had become artistically colored with age. The colors and the way it harmonized into the bark and the way it had all grown over, it was really very, very interesting and not a little bit beautiful. I really feel that by now after all these years it has become a point of historic interest rather than a desecration of nature.

There is one other place in the Tetons where I might have done this. This was when Mr. Owen and I came with the horses up Death Canyon and camped in Alaska Basin. I think this was also when we named it Alaska Basin because it had no name before that. We camped there by a little lake with the horses and I think I may have done some carving there. That was so long ago and the memory is so vague that I doubt if I could find it now and I hope nobody else does.

Chipmunk, Bridger-Teton National Forest photo.

ON ENJOYING THE OUTDOORS

There is a new concept in both trail walking and mountaineering now days. People are doing it more for the sheer pleasure of it.

In the early days on the Teton trails people would come back and brag that they had hiked the Skyline loop trail in a day and a half or just one day. Well, what did that accomplish if it only took them less than two days? They didn't see much. They didn't stop to look at the mountains. They didn't hear the birds singing nor look at the flowers. I don't think they enjoyed it very much. They were collecting fast hikes, just like mountaineers used to collect peaks and first ascents.

I cringe now when somebody says they have made a lot of first ascents. I cringe now when people tell me they have climbed the Grand Teton several hundred times. Because what good is that? The important thing is did they enjoy what they were doing? Did they really have fun? Did they really do something that they liked to do and made them happy and added to the worthwhileness of their existance?

People now are coming to the realization that it is a far better experience to maybe take three days to see one area more thoroughly than to see six times the area very superficially.

Most climbers that I have been acquainted with over the past fifty years, whether they are skilled or unskilled, have been aflicted with the summit collecting ambition. The getting to the summit is the big thing with them. They felt that the trip was not a success unless they reached the top.

I have always tried to counteract that idea in certain respects, but the fact is that I seldom had any failures. The number of failures that I had on the climbs that I attempted would certainly be less than one in fifty. This was mainly because of our planning and the fact that except on very special occasions, I wouldn't take people on fast trips. The day before the climb, we plan very carefully about their conservation of energy and their salt balance and their psychological easiness. We generally tried too, to get into a high enough position before the climb so that we could do the mountain without a horrendously long day.

After my first couple of climbs, I got into the teaching of climbing. I wanted to learn from people if they had been to Switzerland and new anything about climbing or hiking. I learned all I could from them. And I wanted to teach them all I knew if they were interested in learning. It was actually a learning trip which brought on companionship and fun and interest far beyond just climbing up the mountain.

This same philosophy applies to mountaineering, backpacking and hiking. The mountains should be fun. So many people, even yet in these days when we have the techniques of clothing and equipment, still go to the outdoors and hike the trails without really enjoying it. They get blisters and have clothes that are either too hot or too cold. Possibly their camping equipment won't stand the storm or they have inadequate sleeping bags so they are cold at night. If they get wet, they freeze. Or they may hike too fast and get exhausted.

With all this, I'm sure that a lot of young folks taking to the outdoors for the first time think that it's a place to suffer. I know a lot of young guys who have lost their favorite girl friends because they took them out camping to show them what big men they were. So they plan a trip where they hike too far and they exhaust their companion. They even try to climb something where they pull the girl up places where they are scared to death. The judgement factor here is just practically nil.

This reminds me of one of the great tragedies of a fellow I know right here and now. He has his camper and is not necessarily much of a hiker. Almost every weekend he drives to the road end and hikes in to a fishing place. This is his whole life. He married a gal, and this was perhaps twenty years ago, and she was very hesitant about going camping. He had planned the trip very carefully and she wasn't going to have to do a thing. It wasn't going to be a hike, he was going to break her into it very gently. She really didn't want to go. She didn't see much sense in going out there with all those mosquitos and "crawlies" and sleeping in a sleeping bag. She would rather spend their money going out to a dinner or driving to Denver to stay in a nice hotel.

He was going to show her how nice the outdoors really was.

They got to the road end where they were going to make camp and he told her to sit down on a log while he made a little fire for some coffee. He was going to put up the camp while she relaxed over her cup of coffee. He was going to pitch the tent by a tree but there was a limb up there in the way. It was a very dry limb about seven or eight feet long and about as big around as your wrist. He was going to break it off so he pulled that limb back and broke it. Well, a piece of it about a foot long flew back and hit his wife in the mouth, knocking some of her teeth out. I saw the poor fellow last fall going hunting alone. His wife weighs about 200 pounds now and she stays at home. He never got her in the outdoors again.

ABOUT WOMEN IN THE OUTDOORS

The last ten years have changed my mind completely about the role of women in outdoor recreation, mountaineering, hiking, and packpacking. I think we have all been brainwashed to assume that women are not as strong as men. Probably they are not, as far as lifting weights, and men are generally a little larger. But women also have been brainwashed into thinking they can't do things.

Until recently the mores of civilization were such that a lady just didn't do these things. They were taught that they should be in the background, that they should be helped and they were sort of a tender little flower-type to be protected and guarded. They thought it would hurt women if they lifted heavy objects and they would strain themselves. They shouldn't walk long distances, they shouldn't run or carry heavy loads.

Now, on these longer trips where we carry our food for several days, carry full camping equipment in all kinds of weather, also a certain amount of climbing equipment, fishing and photographic equipment as well as clothing for extra tough weather, our packs by real necessity are heavy. We have found that women (this is not a scientific fact but I think that someday it will be generally known) have more endurance than men on the long pull. And we have found them stronger psychologically under stress. There is something about a woman that after they get confidence in themselves, they don't panic. They're not thrown by unusual circumstances. They can make decisions under pressure and they can really carry their load.

That dark-eyed water . . . is it not the first
sign of spring? How its darkness contrasts
with the general lightness at winter!
It has more life in it than any part
of earth's surface. It is where one of the
arteries of the earth is palpable, visible.

—Henry David Thoreau

ON FROZEN FEET

Curly (my brother Eldon) was with me when I made the first winter ascent of the Grand Teton in 1936. The year of this later incident is forgotten but I think it was around 1971.

This was on our New Years climb which we had established as an annual event by then and Curly wanted to go along. He came up from his horse ranch in California and went on the climb with us.

On the day that we made the summit, he had left his felt shoes, (the specially built shoes that we had to climb with during the winter and were very warm) he had left them down below and had on a pair of leather boots. These were large and had three pairs of socks in them. I had to make the decision whether he should turn around and go back and not climb the Grand Teton or whether he would go on up in his leather boots. I made the mistake of letting him continue in those leather boots.

On the way down after making the top, we were in quite a severe storm with the wind blowing 40 or 50 miles an hour and the temperature around 25 below zero. He had to stand in the snow on several occasions. He sort of took over the duty of helping one of the gals down who had become a little bit fatigued and a little frightened on some of the steep snow slopes. He was helping her and that meant that he stood a longer time in the cold snow. But he wasn't particularly cold.

When they got down, he went into the snow cave, crawled into his sleeping bag and went to sleep. He didn't know anything was wrong until the next morning. He woke up and saw that his toes were turning black. (In this leg the whole thing down to the foot is a little bit numb anyway. He was one of the worlds leading jockeys and has had numerous falls on the race track where this leg had been injured at least a couple of times. As a result, it didn't have the feeling that the other leg did.)

When I saw the toe turning black, I knew immediately that there was going to be an amputation. Anybody who has something frozen and gets in the bag and thaws it out and then has to move down off the mountain, there's just hardly any chance of saving the member. My main concern was that we avoided gangrene which there is a great risk of getting in a case like this.

He skied down the mountain and across Bradley Lake. We had sent someone on ahead and the Rangers came up in snowmobiles to the edge of the lake and took him the rest of the way back.

He was very, very fortunate. After a short stay in Jackson, he went to his home in California. His doctor happened to be a young doctor who had been in northern Korea when the Americans were forced to defeat by the Chinese. Hundreds and hundreds of American soldiers were frozen to death or had various parts of their bodies frozen. So instead of amputating the foot, which would have had to have been cut off quite a ways back of the toes, the doctor asked him if he wanted to try a method that had been tried a few times before of just letting the thing fall off by itself and not amputate.

Curly stayed there in the hospital with his foot up for about seven weeks and finally, when they had completely dried up, he just flipped the toes off with his fingers. Consequently, he has the whole ball of his foot and nothing but his toes are missing. He walks around and moves without anyone knowing that his toes are gone.

This experience shows that even people with experience and that know better can still make mistakes.

Paul and brother Eldon on top of the Grand Teton in 1975, Jackson Hole News photo by Q. Jensen.

A NEAR-TRAGIC CLIMB

This is a climbing experience which was route-finding by memory alone, without being able to see anything. This was certainly the closest experience to death that I have ever had in my life and I don't know how we ever got out of it.

This is related to speed on the trails. There was this fellow in the Tetons who was a friend of mine who used to tell us about going to Glacier National Park. I don't suppose the Park Service would allow this now days but he was proud of the fact and bragged of the fact that he could run down mountain sheep and goats. He would just take out after them and claimed that he could catch them. This was almost unbelievable but this guy was a speed demon. He, with another friend of mine, made the famous trip up and down the Grand Teton from Jenny Lake in 3½ hours, or something close to it, running all the way.

I was going to take a friend of mine who was an English Professor at Princeton and another person I know on a guided climb up the Grand Teton. It was very late in the season in September although the weather was good and the mountains had not had any big snows up to that time. This guy wanted to go along with us up the East Ridge but he couldn't leave with us the day before. He said he would come up the next morning and meet us. I said he would have to come early because the best we can do from Surprise Lake to the top of the Grand Teton on the east ridge is ten hours of continuous climbing. Of course in the fall it gets dark early and you don't have the long summer days. So I said that he would have to arrive at a certain time, I think it was three o'clock in the morning.

We waited until about four and he wasn't there so we took off without him, thinking that something had happened and he wasn't coming. We climbed and climbed up the East Ridge of the Grand Teton which is not a climb like the "wall" of Yosemite, but it is from a pure mountaineering standpoint one of the most difficult climbs in America. It has everything on it, a very intricate route up and down around pinnacles, ice and snow climbing, the whole works.

It's quite easy for the first thousand feet or so until you hit those pinnacles. They look like the side of the mountain, but in reality they are cut clear through and you have to go around and down through loose rocks and everything.

We were climbing and making pretty good progress. I guess about two o'clock in the afternoon we were doing allright as we were just traversing the last gendarme, past most of the bad climbing. We heard a voice down below calling in a series of threes. He was yelling something that I couldn't hear but it was in a series of threes. I said "that's old Joe, he's in trouble."

I had to make a decision. I left these people there and because I didn't know what kind of trouble he was in and being afraid that time might run short on us, I took a couple of ropes and ran back down. I took some chances by climbing some difficult pitches without belay but I finally came onto Joe. There he was, spread-eagled on a ledge. He could neither get up nor down. He was trapped.

I threw a rope to Joe. There was no use belittling him—that wouldn't help—until we got him off the mountain. I had to take him on up because I had to get back to the other people. I wasn't about to assume the responsibilty of letting him go back alone, even though he had been running all over the mountains most of his life.

He had been standing on this ledge quite a while, having run all the way up from Jenny Lake, starting about the time he was supposed to meet us at Surprise Lake. He was pretty exhausted and was slow and shaking as we went on up to join the others.

Then a storm came over the mountain and it turned into a blizzard. The snow was blowing directly up those chimneys and the wind was howling. It was just one of those awful fall storms that start out with thunder and lightning and then starts to snow heavily. We were dressed fairly well but we weren't dressed for winter. So—what to do? I knew that if we tried to go down we'd have to bivouac as we were fairly close to the top.

It was a desperate situation and it was getting dark. I didn't think we would last a bivouac in that kind of weather, and so we had to go on. I knew there was no use going over the top. The visibility was practically zero and you couldn't see another fellow ten feet away.

I decided to traverse the mountain so that's what we did. We cut across the roof of that mountain, along a route that I knew crossed the Exum ridge and over to the Owen route. We hit the Owen route just above the upper saddle, right above the rappel and went down that way. Until we reached the lower saddle, at no time could we even see ten feet in front of us.

It was dark and snowing from the time we started the traverse across the top of the mountain. That was a real touch and go situation in every sense of the word. We were able to do that whole thing just because I knew every rock, every crack and every hand hold on that mountain. I must have had a gyro inside of me that night to keep me on course because I had to make it. I knew the slant of the mountain, I knew the elevations and I knew the gullies and the contours of them. I wasn't sure, but I hoped all the time that I knew exactly where we were. It proved out that I did, as we finally came out on the lower saddle. Totally exhausted, we spent the night in some sleeping bags I had left there before.

That was the extreme example of difficult route-finding and I doubt very much if I could ever do it again.

Top of Grand Teton and Mt. Owen, Bridger-Teton National Forest photo by Perkins.

ON GIVING DIRECTIONS

I've found during my life that drawing things on a map and telling people about trails is certainly no guarantee that they are going to follow those trails and not get lost. I remember one time there was a group of friends of mine from the east that wanted to do what we call the Skyline Trail. It goes up Cascade Canyon and all the way around on the ridge and comes out Death Canyon. I was going to pick them up when they came out of Death Canyon to the White Grass Ranch and called me at Jenny Lake.

They were going to make the trip in three or four days. This much time passed, then five days passed, and then six, and I was getting desperate wondering where they were. Finally, I got a call from Victor, Idaho and that's where they were. They had gotten completely lost and had gotten down a little far on the Idaho side, so they followed some of the canyons down. They followed the old admonition that when lost, follow a stream down and eventually you'll reach civilization.

I had gone to great, great pains to not only mark this trail on the map but had put little notes on it on what they were to see and where they were to turn and how long it would take from here to there, and they still ended up in Victor, Idaho.

*Nature is not benevolent; Nature is just, gives
pound for pound, measure for measure, makes
no exceptions, never tempers her decrees with
mercy, or winks at any infringement of her laws . . .
It is a hard gospel; but rocks are hard too,
yet they form the foundations of the hills.*

—John Burroughs

ON WEATHER AND GETTING LOST

When people look at trails and they have a map and know that they are going to stay on the trails, they perhaps think that they are not going to get lost and are not going to get into serious trouble. Lots of times the way that they get in trouble is by not knowing what a storm will mean or not knowing how the time element and elevation will affect them.

This story is about one of the big mountaineering clubs of America that came to the Tetons for an outing. This is a classical one. They arrived in their cars at Jenny Lake and everyone was anxious to get out and do something right away.

It was about noon and the group decided they would hike up to Surprise Lake and be back for supper—it's only four and a half miles. A couple of the people said they would stay down and take care of the camp and have supper ready when the rest got back. But it was four and a half miles and three thousand vertical feet to the lake. They had just arrived from back east and hadn't been acclimated and had been riding in cars several days. They had a lot of spirit but little endurance.

Well, by the time they reached Surprise Lake, it was dusk. And then a huge thunderstorm came up. It rained like a cloudburst. They stood under the big trees trying to keep dry. By the time they started down the switchbacks from Surprise Lake, it was dark and still raining and they couldn't see their hands in front of their faces. Two of the leaders said they would run down and be sure that the bedding was dried out and tend to the things that needed attention in camp. So they went on ahead.

They had supper and everything ready and they waited, and waited, and waited and nobody arrived. So they got real worried and got some flashlights and ran back up the trail through the night, calling as they ran, practially all the way back to Surprise Lake—no people.

The group at the lake had started down the switchbacks below the lake. One of the switchbacks continues on over to Bradley Lake, if you miss where the main trail cuts back on its way to Jenny Lake where they came from. So, suddenly they saw a lake and realized that they hadn't seen any lake on the way up. By that time the clouds and rain had lifted a little and they could look out towards the east and they could see cars out there on the highway. That seemed a perfect solution—to walk to the highway, not knowing that there was enroute lots of downed timber, and about a mile of mosquito swamps and beaver ponds. And so they got into the beaver ponds and while going through the downed timber and swamps they got separated into groups of three or four. Along about daylight they came to the Cottonwood River which was too big to cross. They had to walk up the river through trail-less and brushy country, which brought them practically all the way back to Jenny Lake before they could get across the river.

They dragged into camp about eight o'clock in the morning, absolutely exhausted, bitten by mosquitos, and with moss from the beaver ponds hanging on their clothes. They were only going to stay for a week and it took them two more days to get rested up. A lot of them had to leave without even getting up Symmetry Spire after planning to climb the Grand Teton, Mt. Morran, Mt. Owen and several other peaks.

Yellow Violet, Bridger-Teton National Forest photo.

ON LOSING YOUR DIRECTION

Ordinarily there's practically no need for a compass in mountains like the Tetons because you always know what drainage you're in. However, on the other side in Targhee Forest where you have eight or ten miles of flat country in heavy timber, if you get turned around that can be a different story. You just can't see out above the trees to the peaks you would recognize. Here a compass would be quite helpful if one got off the trail.

One time that I was really confused was when I was following one trail when I thought I was on another. This was in a snow storm when suddenly the clouds parted and I saw the Snake River down below that I knew had to be north of me. That was an awful feeling to see that river south of me when I knew it should be to the north. Then I had to sit down and try to figure where camp was. I finally got myself straightened out but it really shook me up to get turned around like that in these mountains that I know like the back of my hand.

ON GETTING TURNED AROUND

I have gotten to the point in these mountains where I can generally see a peak and know where I am. I haven't pulled out a compass in thirty years. Even though it's fogged in, I know the contours and I know the rivers.

It think it was about 1972, going on our winter ascent of the Grand Teton, that I lost the whole group. I was really sort of embarrassed. This was at the beginning on the way to Bradley Lake before you even get into Garnet Canyon. There were marks on the trees but the trails were snowed under. However, I wasn't necessarily trying to follow the trail because in the winter time the best terrain for skiing is not necessarily right along the trail. There is a system of ridges along through those woods on the morraine and there are lots of humps in there. I knew where Bradley Lake was, so I just went cross-country knowing full well that I could hit the lake.

It was snowing so you couldn't see the mountains but we were making pretty good time. Finally, I figured we must be about there. Suddenly I heard a snowmobile quite close. Then I realized that I had come about a mile and a half back towards the valley. If I hadn't heard that machine, I would have made a complete loop back to where we started. That was certainly a great shock to me.

I will arise and go now, for always night and day
I hear lake water lapping with low sounds by the shore
While I stand on the roadway, or on the pavements grey,
I hear it in the deep heart's core.

— W. B. Yeats

.CUMMING 76

ON POACHING

In the early days of Jackson Hole, even as late as the time I started ranching there in the middle thirties, it was a common practice and it was considered a privilege by the ranchers to kill deer, elk and moose as much as they needed for their winter supply. Without refrigeration the only way they had to keep meat was to wait until the weather was cold enough so it would freeze by itself.

After the hunting season was over, we used to go out and shoot five of six elk and maybe a moose. If you got the meat in November during the cold weather and they froze, you could hang them in the barn or an outside shed where they would be protected from the sun and the warming temperatures of the day. That meat would last until March or April.

I can remember talking to one of the game wardens about his early day experiences of game wardening. One time he told about going down to the southern part of Jackson Hole and out the Snake River Canyon to attempt to get the people around Afton, Alpine and Swan Valley to stop their poaching practices. Those people there figured that they helped feed the game in the winter and were entitled to shoot what they needed for themselves. He decided to have a show down with them, even at the risk of his life. He planned to have the first man he arrested to be a man of some substance and standing in the area. So the first man that he arrested there was a Mormon bishop. He made the charges stick, so that sort of started game law and order in that country.

Up in the Tetons on the Idaho side the state line is not at the base of the mountains but half way up the mountains. The trails on that side went up through the timber for sometimes eight or ten miles and then hit the Wyoming border and went on up to the crest of the ridge. Then they crossed over to the east and dropped down into Jackson Hole. The people of Jackson Hole never came over on the other side to hunt because they had plenty of hunting on their own side of the mountain.

The people living on the Idaho side went up on the mountain and hunted all the time. The great hunting always took place before haying and the harvesting season. They would go up there to get deer, elk and moose and bring them down to feed their harvesting crew. In those days there was a lot of hand work in harvesting and a big crew needed a lot of meat. After the game wardens started coming over they had to devise ways to get the meat they needed and still avoid the wardens. This is when this thing with the pack horses started.

They would go up near the ridge of the mountains, which would be in Wyoming, and shoot their game. Then they loaded the meat on their big pack horses that knew their way home. At dusk they would turn the pack horses loose to make their way back to the barn. The riders would wash all traces of the meat from themselves and ride "clean" down the trail back to their ranch in Idaho. They knew when they got home the pack horses would be standing outside the corral waiting to get in. The game warden said if he took out after one of those pack horses it was practically impossible to catch them. Whenever he would get close, they would head through the timber, off the trails through the brush. The Idaho side was too isolated to have any Idaho wardens so if these Wyoming wardens didn't catch the pack horses while they were still up on the Wyoming part of the mountain, they were home free.

This practice went on for quite a while and according to some it still prevails to some extent.

Tetons, Bridger-Teton National Forest photo by Scott Phillips.

Introduction to the Tetons

Hiking and backpacking in the Tetons as well as other places is enjoyed most by those who have learned how to get along in the wild outdoors. There are a great many things that one can learn to help him enjoy his outdoors experiences. I have covered these in my book "The Wilderness Handbook" which I recommend to anyone wishing detailed information about most outdoor situations. However, for this hiking and backpacking guide to the Tetons, I will briefly review and summarize some of those things which I feel will help you enjoy the Tetons as I have.

To begin with, as most of the trails in the Tetons start at the bottom of canyons and generally climb to the ridges and peaks, and only a few traverse on the level for any great distance, I have devised a rating system which will combine the miles hiked and the elevation gained into an equivalent value of horizontal miles. Since climbing vertically 500 feet uses the same energy as hiking one mile on the level, if you gained 500 feet in elevation after hiking one mile, this would be the equivalent of hiking two miles on level ground. This one mile hike would then be energy rated "two miles". The actual miles and energy rated miles (E.R.) are given at the beginning of each hike. This will assist any hiker to judge the hike in terms of his own ability. Whether or not you are wearing a pack, this rating system will work the same. If you know your capabilities on level ground, this will translate your energy needs to the mountain trail.

TRIP CONSIDERATIONS

I believe that the experiences of being in the mountains hiking, camping, or climbing are fun and should be enjoyed. In order to enjoy a trip, a person must know that he will be safe and be able to complete the trip. In order to protect those on a trip, there are three main things I would like to consider: weather, time, and energy.

WEATHER

In high mountain country such as the Tetons, it is imperative that one knows ahead of time what weather he is likely to encounter on the trip. He can then plan for the type of equipment he must carry, such as clothing, tents and sleeping bag. Naturally, if he can expect below freezing nights, he would take different equipment than if he could expect balmy days and nights.

The weather information required would vary with the length of the trip planned. A half day trip would require little more than a radio forecast. One must always keep in mind that the Tetons generate their own weather and quick changes can be expected. With this in mind, one can gather weather information for longer trips. The best way to get this is to call the U.S. Weather Bureau.

What you need to know is the average day and night temperatures and the probable weather you will encounter. Ask about the past history of rain or snow and percentage of stormy days for this area at this time of year. With this information about what the weather will probably be, with the past history of what it has been, you can judge fairly well what it might be for the duration of your trip.

It would be impractical to be prepared for the very worst that could happen. This would entail carrying such amounts of clothing and equipment as to make the trip unenjoyable if not downright impossible. I have found that by being prepared for a little worse weather than which was predicted enabled me to safely sit out the worst storms.

TIME CONTROL

For every trip whether it be a day hike or a lengthy expedition, one needs to know when he plans to leave and far more important, when he will return. Several things determine the length of the trip such as the distances involved, type of terrain to be covered, and ability of the people involved. After considering all these things, a time schedule is set up, even if it's only the time agreed upon to return. Parents or relatives are told when to expect us and agencies governing the area visited need this information. If we don't show up on schedule people worry and possibly costly rescue operations are begun. Therefore, it is imperative that we have time control in order to predict accurately when we will come back.

Using judgement in planning for the unexpected and being flexible in our plans helps much in keeping to a schedule. One should check the progress frequently and set new goals depending on the preceeding day's achievements. To more thoroughly enjoy an outing, one should be trip oriented rather than destination oriented. This means enjoy the experience as you go along and be prepared to abandon efforts to get to the top if it's becoming clear that you won't make it with the present progress. It is far better to allow for too much time than not enough, as a more leisurely trip will be more pleasant for the extra time to hear the birds or watch the changing scenery. John Ruskin said: "There was always more in the world than a man could see, walked he ever so slowly. He will see no more if he goes fast."

ENERGY CONTROL

A great many mountaineering accidents are caused by the person becoming overly tired. This is often caused by their not knowing how to develop and conserve body energy. They do not eat or drink properly and push themselves through being anxious or nervous. Frequently accidents happen on the way down a mountain because the person is too tired to remain alert to hazardous terrain.

One should be prepared physically if the trip will be long or strenuous. On a trip a person must never allow himself to become exhausted. Energy and stamina should be built and rationed by judicious use of proper trail techniques and practicing methods that develop and sustain strength.

Ones physical condition has to be developed before one sets

out on the trail. In the office or at home the stairs can be used to develop muscles in the legs and heart. Walk (don't run) either up or down from one to three steps at a time. Deep breathing exercises will increase lung capacity and prepare one for high altitude walking. Isometric exercises can be done at the desk or in a car. These can be the pushing of arms or legs against fixed objects or each other.

CONSERVING ENERGY

The energy needed to hike in the mountains can be likened to driving a car in the mountains, shifting gears up or down as the steepness of the road dictates.

The rate of breathing and heart beat are good indications of our body's rate of energy use. As the breathing is easiest to measure, we'll refer to it in this comparison. To conserve energy and power a car motor should run at about the same speed all the time. Some cars have tachometers to indicate the correct speed to shift gears to get the most efficient use. Of course, you know the steeper the climb, the lower the gear to keep the motor running the same speed.

Hiking on the level, our breathing maintains the same rhythmic cycle, so many steps to each breath whether we are conscious of it or not. We should recognize this and determine what our rhythmic cycle is—say, three steps breathing in and three steps breathing out. Now the real conservation of energy comes when you start to gain altitude on a trail. Remember, the most efficient use of your energy is to keep your motor (heart) running at about the same speed all the time. Therefore, as you start breathing faster, take less steps for each breath. If you are still breathing too rapidly after "gearing down" to one step inhale, one step exhale, take shorter steps.

After practicing this rhythmic breathing, you will find yourself much less tired at the end of the day.

Keeping ones body strength at a constant level is very important in conserving ones energy. A frequent intake of both food and water is necessary to maintain this level. It is far better to have several small snacks than to have only two or three larger meals. One should never get hungry or thirsty in the mountains as loss of strength or dehydration can occur quickly and could be disastrous if you're in a dangerous situation such as trying to get off a mountain ahead of a heavy storm.

Through perspiration we lose both body moisture and salt. At high elevations this loss is much quicker and may go unnoticed. The amount of salt in foods is seldom sufficient to replace that lost due to perspiration. Salt tablets or salt crystals should be taken regularly, about one tablet for each pint of water consumed.

Proper clothing is necessary to conserve ones energy and enjoy the mountains. One should always feel comfortable, otherwise he is not properly dressed. If one gets too warm, energy is lost through excessive perspiration. If one is chilled, blood is withdrawn from the outer extremities to warm the inner body and he gets even colder and may suffer frostbite. The layer affect is best for clothing. Several light layers are used and put on or taken off as needed.

I enter some glade in the woods, perchance,
where a few weeds and dry leaves alone
lift themselves above the surface of the snow . . .
This is what I go out to seek.
It is as if I always met in those places
some grand, serene, immortal, infinitely encouraging,
though invisible, companion,
and walked with him.

—Henry David Thoreau

CLOTHING

In dressing for the Tetons as for any other high mountain country there are three main things to consider: insulation, ventilation, and protection against the elements. You must be prepared for sudden rainstorms, hail, and frequently snow around the tops of the peaks. It is well known in the area that the Tetons can and do manufacture their own weather. Storms are generated in those mountains that cannot be predicted from what's happening in surrounding areas. A period of prolonged sunny weather is no guarantee that it will continue for the duration of your trip. One who plans only for good weather could be risking the success of the trip and even his life.

Backpackers usually plan for possible changes in the weather but a very important rule for those taking day hikes in the Tetons is that one should dress or carry clothing so he could survive one night on the mountain should he become injured, lost or otherwise unable to make it back the same day.

In cold weather, a good head covering is a must as a great deal of body heat can be lost by exposing the head to the wind. A wool stocking cap is best for this situation as it can also be pulled down over the ears when needed. In warm sunny weather a hat with a brim to prevent sunburn is needed as the clear mountain air produces sunburn much quicker than the heavier polluted air found at lower elevations.

A light wind and rain parka should be carried in the Tetons. Even on sunny days you may become chilled while exposed to a strong wind on an exposed peak or high ridge. The outer material should be water repellant but not waterproof. A waterproof material will shed the rain but also retain body perspiration to such an extent that you may become soaking wet from the inside if you are hiking through the rain.

A good tightly woven wool shirt can serve both as a wind breaker and a rain parka in milder storms. Wool has exceptional properties that make it ideal for use in the mountains. It has natural oils that make it somewhat rainproof. It traps the air to provide good insulation. It keeps a person warm even when it gets wet. It conducts perspiration moisture away from the skin to outer layers of clothing where it

Old Stump, Bridger-Teton National Forest photo by Scott
Phillips

evaporates. It allows ventilation to occur so undue perspiration is not induced. The wool shirt should be extra long to cover the midriff while bending or reaching and also be open at the neck with buttons to allow adjustments to heat conditions.

A loose knit sweater is a valuable addition to ones outdoor attire. This may sometimes be worn under the shirt and at other times by itself. Some people complain of itching and scratching when wearing wool next to the skin. This could be cause by several things. Some wool is woven with the ends sticking out rather than woven into the fabric. Soap used in washing the garment is difficult to rinse out and could cause irritation of the skin. Natural wool softness can be destroyed by boiling temperatures while washing. Some kinds of wool are preferable when it is to be worn next to the skin: lamb's wool, cashmere, or virgin wool. Try these if you feel you are allergic to wool.

Cotton pants or shorts are more comfortable than wool on hot days but to rely on them completely in the Tetons could be disastrous. A tough tightly woven pair of trousers is best for mountain wear. A pair of nylon wind pants is valuable to wear in cold windy places as wool will not keep the wind out under these circumstances. Rain pants of a waterproof material are of little value as their lack of ventilation makes them unsuited for prolonged hiking.

Wool socks are a must for use in the high Teton country. A 75 percent wool blend with nylon may be used in the summer. A loose weave is preferable to allow moisture to escape more easily. It is better to wear two pair of wool socks as this not only keeps the foot warmer but also allows movement between the feet and boot with less chance of blisters. Your feet will stay dryer as wool conducts moisture away from the feet. Lighter summer boots may have room for only one pair of socks. You can either go with two pair of light wool socks or just one pair of heavier ones. Those who feel they can't wear the coarse wool socks against their feet can get a light fine wool sock to put on first. A cotton sock worn next to the foot will get wet quickly from perspiration, stick to the foot with each movement and cause blisters.

A good pair of boots is the most important part of your

outdoor equipment. If your feet hurt there is no way that you can enjoy a trip into the mountains. The use of tennis shoes or street shoes with thin soles is hard on the feet as each rock on a mountain trail can be felt. The constant bending and twisting of soft soled shoes puts a strain on the ligaments and bones of the foot that they are not accustomed to. This will cause severe pain on a trip of any length. Climbers use a thick soled hard boot similar to a ski boot to allow them to put their entire weight on only the edge to support them on a small ledge or projection. A little climbing is usually done on most hiking trails so a modified boot is needed that is a compromise between the heavy climbing boot and a light walking shoe. For most hiking on rocky trails one needs a sole that will bend for comfortable walking yet be thick enough to withstand sharp pointed rocks. In general the heavier the person and pack he carries, the thicker the sole needed. Vibram lugged soles are necessary on all but the smooth level trails.

Boots must fit properly to be comfortable. Most boot problems are caused by boots that are too tight. When buying a boot, have them fitted with the same amount of socks you will be wearing in the mountains. The boot should fit loosely as it will be better ventilated, stay drier and warmer and cause fewer blisters. Try the boot on in your bare feet without lacing it. Push your toes forward as far as possible and bend at the knees. There should be enough room to put your finger between your heel and the back of the boot without pressure. A larger person should have half-again that space.

A new boot can cause pain and blisters if not broken in before extensive use. The easiest way is to fill the boots with water for a few minutes and then wear the wet boot. This will allow the softened leather to conform to your foot. Water will not harm your boots. If they become wet through use, they should be allowed to dry naturally.

CAMPING FOR CONSERVATION

Perhaps one can remember a hiking trip in past years when he came across a small lake back in the mountains that gave every evidence of not ever having been visited by another human being. Grass and flowers grew lush to the waters edge, no black rings scarred the shore nor axe marks showed on the trees to give evidence of former campers. Remember how you enjoyed the feeling there of pristine nature, the same feeling that you try to experience on every hiking trip but with less and less success each succeeding year. Each person coming into the mountains is seeking for this feeling. With hundreds and now thousands of people going into the mountains, we are in danger of completely destroying the wilderness feeling through lack of knowledge of how to camp without damage to the ecosystem.

The basic thing to remember is to camp and pass through an area and leave no trace of your having been there. Going one step further, camp so that at that moment you are not obvious through sight or sound to others in the same area. This means camp well away from lakes and trails and other campers. There is always an abundance of excellent camping places within a short walking distance of a lake or trail. Camp by a small stream or spring, or carry a plastic pail to bring water from the lake. Save the lake as a place to take a walk and meditate and commune with nature, unmarred by the sights and sounds of multicolored tents and campers blocking your free access around the lake.

In many places in the wilderness, no open fires are permitted. This has become necessary mainly because of damage to trees in the area as firewood becomes more and more scarce. Careless or unthinking campers chop down almost everything that will burn, leaving unsightly stumps and scars all around. The highest form of conservation camping is to use only a small stove with self contained fuel. There are numerous kinds on the market to meet any need. If one must have a campfire (no one can deny the feeling of friendship that sitting around an open fire can bring) one should select a place where there is an abundance of available firewood and use it in such a way that you leave no trace of you're having been there. This means preparing a fire hole in a safe place and then covering it up with the same sod before leaving.

Washing dishes should be done away from streams and lakes where food particles and soap residue won't contaminate the water. A sump hole can be dug for wash water, where all traces can be covered up.

Latrines should be located on high ground well away from any stream or lake. For groups a larger hole should be dug and the shovel left nearby so dirt can be thrown in after each use. Another good practice for groups is to place a shovel and a role of toilet paper at the edge of camp so each person knows it's there to use. In each case, whether you dig one larger hole or individual holes, the depth of the hole is important. It should not be deep into the mineral soil as decomposition is very slow there. Rather, dig down eight or ten inches and after use cover it over with natural humus. Decay will convert it to soil in a year's time.

The disposing of garbage is important in order to leave a clean campsite. The general rule is to burn all the burnables and carry out everything else. Nothing should be buried, tucked under rocks or thrown back into the bushes out of sight. These things are dug up by rodents, washed out by the rain or appear with the falling of leaves from the bushes. It is good practice to repack all food supplies as much as possible into burnable containers.

Years ago it was common practice to cut pine boughs to use under ones bed. Of course this destructive practice could not long be tolerated with today's heavy use of the forests. It is certainly a very poor conservation practice, so much so that it is now illegal in most forests. Another poor practice is to dig a trench around a tent to carry off excess rain water.

This also falls under the category of "old time" practices which cannot be condoned now. Digging the trench not only destroys plant and tree roots, but leaves an unsightly scar in the earth that takes many years to remove. Doing this is certainly not the way to conserve the wilderness by "leaving no trace that you have been there".

43

SUMMER SNOW TECHNIQUES

High in the peaks of the Tetons one will encounter glaciers or snow fields all summer. Walking on the snow in the summer is much different than in the winter. Snow is usually fairly soft in the winter and should you fall while walking across a slope, the soft snow will stop you. The warm days of summer causes the snow to get moist, with a resultant settling and freezing at night. Should you fall while crossing a snow slope, you could very quickly speed out of control and be dashed against rocks or trees below with serious consequences.

Only cleated soled shoes or boots should be worn if you plan to cross any steep snow slopes on your hike. Smooth soles or tennis shoes could be the cause of a serious accident. A traverse can be made by walking on the edges of the boot. Going up hill you kick steps in the snow with the toes. Going down hill you walk on the heels.

If you plan to encounter many large steep snowfields, you should carry an ice axe and know how to make a "self arrest" should you fall. In extremely dangerous situations you should be roped together as well as be prepared to make self-arrest. Snow fields and glaciers contain hidden dangers and the best precaution is to avoid them if they appear to be dangerous.

If no one knows the importance of preserving a beautiful place, that place is not likely to be preserved, but instead transformed to something else and probably something less. . . . The measure of enlightenment will be man's ability in the special places to recognize that the natural things which are there already are good things. These we inherit.

—Ansel Adams

Teton Range

Grand Teton and Mt. Owen from Cascade Canyon
Bridger-Teton National Forest photo by Scott Phillips

Grand Teton National Park

HIKING AND BACKCOUNTRY CAMPING

Grand Teton has over 200 miles of trails that cover a variety of lengths, difficulties, and areas. For those with only a small amount of time, there are self-guiding nature trails at Colter Bay, Cunningham's Cabin, Oxbow Bend, and Menor's Ferry. For those with more time, stamina, and a bit of adventuresome spirit, there are all-day hikes and hikes that can stretch from overnight to several nights in the more remote sections of the Park. Some of these trails are moderate enough that young and old may follow them with a reasonable amount of exertion. The beginning elevation for most trails is 6,800 feet so consideration to physical condition and age should be given and those from lower altitudes should go easy. Exhaustion comes quickly at this altitude.

Trail conditions
The high country trails are usually snow covered until early July, whereas the trails on the valley floor are generally free of snow by mid-June. Ice axes are generally required for safe passage of Static Peak and Paintbrush Divides until late July. Hurricane, Mount Meek, and Fox Creek Passes can be safely crossed without ice axes up to two weeks before the others, however, snow conditions vary each year and predictions of when the snows will melt are difficult.

Rules of the trail
Horse parties have the right-of-way on trails. Hikers should get well clear of the trail and remain quiet as they pass.
Pets, motorized equipment, wheeled vehicles, firearms or explosive devices are not allowed in the backcountry, on or off the trails.
When photographing or approaching wildlife, use caution, keep at a safe distance and do not molest or feed the animals.

Day hiking

All persons hiking the various trails are asked to register at the trail registration boxes located at each trail head. Information recorded will help in the management of the backcountry by giving indications as to type and quantity of use. If you plan to travel off the established trails or mountain climb, you must register in advance at the Jenny Lake Ranger Station.

Overnight camping

A written, non-fee permit is required for all overnight backcountry use. This permit is available at the Moose Visitor Center, which is open all year, or at Jenny Lake Ranger Station and Colter Bay Visitor Center during the summer months.

The demand of people desiring a wilderness experience is far above the available supply of wilderness in Grand Teton. To preserve and protect the land and to enhance the camping experience, definite backcountry user capacities have been set and are not exceeded. This results in some people being turned away.

Reservations may be made for some of the backcountry camping areas with 30% of these areas available for this purpose; the rest are issued on a first-come, first-served basis. Reserved permits must be picked up by noon of the day the trip begins. First-come, first served sites are not available until the day before the start of the trip. Camping permits must be picked up in person and are not available by mail.

Lonesome Splendor, Jackson Hole News photo by G. Bellerose

*The tempered light of the woods is like a perpetual
morning, and is stimulating and heroic. The anciently
reported spells at these places creep on us . . . . The
incommunicable trees begin to persuade us to live
with them and quit our life of solemn trifles.*

—Ralph Waldo Emerson

SEEING WILDLIFE IN GRAND TETON NATIONAL PARK

Leisurely travel, some understanding of animal habits, and a pair of binoculars, all aid in seeing wildlife. It is hoped that the following comments will also assist you to see and enjoy the rich variety of mammals and birds living in Grand Teton National Park. Wildlife is constantly moving about. Some movements are seasonal and some governed by the time of day. Other factors, such as weather or food, may dictate where animals may be found.

Moose are large mammals, conspicuous at any season. In spring, they frequently feed in open ponds, favorite locations being Blacktail Ponds, northwest of Blacktail Butte; the Sawmill Ponds, along the Wilson Road; Moose Ponds, just south of Jenny Lake; and the Oxbow Bend, west of the Wildlife Range. Many browse in the Willow Flats near Jackson Lake Lodge. During summer, moose move into the spruce and cottonwood forests along the river bottoms. These may be seen by scanning the river bottoms from the scenic overlooks along the Rockefeller Parkway. In fall and winter, the moose move into open country where they are easily observed. It is well to remember that moose are animals of uncertain temperament. One should be especially cautious of cows with calves.

Elk are more shy than moose and for this reason more difficult to see. In addition, elk usually rest in deep forest during mid-day, so early morning and late afternoon are the best times to observe this member of the deer family. During the first half of May, large groups of elk move across Antelope Flats east of the Rockefeller Parkway in their annual return to their summering grounds. For the next month, the cows are more solitary, seeking heavy cover for bearing their calves. Favorite calving areas are Burnt Ridge, Signal Mountain and vicinity, and Timbered Island. The older bulls, for the most part, usually move on north into Yellowstone or to the higher elevations of the Teton Range.

In July and August, elk frequent the area between Signal Mountain and Burnt Ridge. If one drives along one of the gravel roads in this area and quietly parks his car, elk can be seen either about sunup or sundown, moving out of the forest onto the open flats.

Moose and the Tetons, Jackson Hole News photo

Fall is the season when the mature bulls round up their harems of cows. At this time of year, the elk are most easily observed and most exciting to watch. The area about Signal Mountain and Burnt Ridge is still the best part of the park to watch their activity and to hear the challenging bugle of the bulls. Lupine Meadows and Timbered Island are also rewarding places to watch elk.

In early winter, the time depending on snow and weather, large bands of elk again will move across the open flats to their wintering area south of the park.

Mule deer are most often seen by the visitor who hikes the park trails. In summer, the deer prefer the lower mountain slopes. In spring and fall, they are moving between the mountain slopes and their wintering grounds, mostly south of Jackson. Because of deep snow, few deer winter in the park.

Bison (Buffalo) are sometimes seen in the Potholes area or along the Snake River in the vicinity of Moran Junction.

Bighorn (Mountain Sheep) are found in the park in limited numbers. They are most often seen from the trail over the Mount Hunt Divide, between Open and Granite Canyons. In spring and fall, look for them in the vicinity of Gros Ventre Slide just east of the park.

Pronghorn (Antelope) occur in small bands on Antelope Flats during the summer months north of Kelly. They do not winter in this area.

Black Bear are seen occasionally along the lower mountain trails. A few wander into campgrounds and picnic areas. In these locations, they may become a nuisance. When this happens, they are live-trapped and moved to more remote places. In all circumstances, do not approach or feed bears. They are wild animals capable of causing a person severe injury.

Trumpeter Swans can be seen on Christian Pond, east of Jackson Lake Lodge during all but the cold winter months when the pond is covered with ice. During the winter months, they must move about to find open water and food. Blacktail Ponds is a favorite wintering spot.

White Pelicans migrate through the park spring and fall. They often stop at Oxbow Bend.

Ducks and Geese are common along the Snake River and on beaver ponds at all seasons when the ponds are free of ice.

For more details on seeing wildlife, you may wish to consult with a Park Naturalist. A printed check-list of the park's vertebrates may be secured at any of the park's information desks free of charge.

THE ZONE CONCEPT VS. DESIGNATED CAMPING SITES

To allow a freer choice in camping, the Teton Range above 7,000 feet has been divided into camping areas or zones. Campers may stay anywhere within a zone if they follow a few simple rules:

1. No ground fires are allowed. Small backpacking stoves are recommended for cooking purposes.
2. Camp at least 50 feet away from lakes and streams. Try to camp out of sight of the trail or other campers. Do not camp in fragile or overused sites that will show signs of your camp having been there.
3. All materials carried into the backcountry must be carried out. Leave or bury nothing in the backcountry except human feces. Use pit toilets where available, otherwise shallowly bury body wastes away from water, trails and campsites.

NON-ZONED AREAS
Camper carrying capacities have been assigned to all backcountry areas, zoned and non-zoned. Non-zoned camping is allowed for cross-country trips and mountaineering bivouacs only. No reservations will be taken for non-zoned areas. The same restrictions apply here as to zoned camping. Capacities will not be exceeded and may result in some people being turned away.

GROUP CAMPING
Group camping is limited to one night per zone in June, July and August. Group size may not exceed 20 persons and groups are not allowed to break into smaller parties to occupy

Bull Moose, Bridger-Teton National Forest photo.

individual sites. Organized groups are required to obtain a free Special Use Permit from the Superintendent at least one week in advance of their trip and are limited to the number of nights per year they may occupy the backcountry. Group regulations are stricter because of the rapidly increasing demand for backcountry by all users, but particularly organizations and commercial groups.

DESIGNATED SITES

A few designated camping sites still remain below the 7,000 foot level. They are on Jackson, Bearpaw, Trapper, Leigh, and Phelps Lakes only. Wood fires are allowed in the grates provided at these sites only.

CLOSED AREAS

No overnight camping is permitted at Lake Solitude, Bradley Lake, Taggart Lake, Laurel Lake, Amphitheater Lake, and below the Forks of Cascade Creek to Jenny Lake. All other areas of the high country are available for camping, as long as user capacity limits are not exceeded.

WEATHER AND CLOTHING
Summer weather in the mountains is changeable with warm sunny days and cool evenings. Afternoon storms are frequent, especially in June and August. Have a sweater or jacket for evening wear. A light, water-repellent jacket is advisable. Fall provides a good time for hiking, with cooler weather and fewer people. The nights are below freezing and campers should be prepared for frosty mornings that warm slowly. Plenty of dry, warm clothing is essential at this time of year. Exposure sickness (hypothermia) from cold can unexpectedly overcome a hiker soaked by a mountain shower. Carry rain gear and at least the minimum clothing suggested for the season. The mountain stove can quickly heat drinking water to counteract the chill.

WATER
Surface water is of questionable purity, as it is in any place where there are many people.

GUIDE SERVICES
Mountaineering guide service is available at the Exum Guide Service and School of American Mountaineering, a park concession located at Jenny Lake. For information contact Mr. Glenn Exum, Box 103, Moose, WY 83012. Jackson Hole Mountain Guides bases at Teton Village, WY 83025 also offers guide services within the Park.

BACKCOUNTRY CAMPING ZONES AVAILABLE FOR RESERVATION

Surprise Lake	10	Open Canyon	10
Lower Paintbrush	15	Granite to Mt. Hunt	10
Holly Lake	20	Marion Lake	20
Upper Paintbrush	20	No. Fork Granite	25
No. Fork Cascade	20	So./Mdl. Forks Granite	40
So. Fork Cascade	45	Lower Granite	25
Death Canyon	50		

Numbers are maximum capacities for each zone. Alaska Basin is outside Grand Teton in Targhee National Forest. There are no restrictions on camping (no fires allowed).

Phone 307-733-2880 for further information (Moose Ranger Station).

*In Europe, people talk a great deal of the wilds
of America, but the Americans themselves never think
about them; they are insensible to the wonders of
inanimate nature and they may be said not to
perceive the mighty forests that surround them till
they fall beneath the hatchet.*

—Alexis de Tocqueville

Teton National Park Trails

Note: The trail distances are given in miles and Energy Rated (E.R.) miles. For each 500 feet of elevation gained, one mile is added to the distance. The result (E.R.) combines the actual miles with the climbing, to indicate the energy needed for each trail.

AMPHITHEATER LAKE TRAIL

USGS Maps: Moose, Grand Teton
Distances: Surprise Lake 4.6 miles, E.R. 10.2 miles.
            Amphitheater Lake 4.8 miles, E.R. 10.7 miles.

Amphitheater and Surprise Lakes are very popular one day hikes in Grand Teton National Park. They are one day hikes that might exhaust you, not because of the mileage that's traversed, but because of the amount of altitude that is gained. You start out on the trail from a place called Lupine Meadows parking area. You can reach this parking area by going about 7 miles above the Moose Headquarters of Grand Teton National Park towards Jenny Lake or just about ¾ of a mile south from the South Jenny Lake Junction where the road splits to go to Jenny Lake. There a dirt road goes down the hill, crosses Cottonwood Creek on a wooden bridge and goes about two miles over to Lupine Meadows where you can park your car.

Lupine Meadows is not a place where one can camp over night. Over night camping would be in one of the camp grounds at Jenny Lake or over on the Gros Ventre. A person can drive from Jackson up to this starting place in less than an hour.

There's a Ranger Station at Jenny Lake and information can be secured there. Or if one is coming from the south, information can be secured at the park headquarters at Moose. Generally they don't require a sign out or a registration on one day hikes, but it's always best if one has time or unless one knows what the regulations are to stop at one of the Ranger

Stations where one can get information. Registration at the Jenny Lake Ranger Station is required for any off-trail hiking and for climbing.

This is an excellent trail and it's a wide trail. It was one of the good trails that was built by the CCC's back in the early 1930's and the old CC camp used to be there near Jenny Lake. Some of the buildings are still there. One of them is used by the Mountaineering Concession which is now operated by Glen Exum, the first guide that I ever trained in the Tetons. He started to climb for me in 1928 and these old buildings are still the headquarters of the Climbing School that Glen now operates.

In starting out on this hike, you go over a log rip-rap that goes across a swamp and then you hit a trail that climbs very gradually to the south about a mile over to where one can look down into Burned Wagon Gulch to the south. There is a timber blow down through here, but it has been cleared from the trail. The great fall of timber was caused in 1973 by a terrific wind that swept down off the Tetons. It was sort of a down draft wind that is not uncommon to this country, but this was one of greater magnitude than they've had before and it knocked down literally hundreds of thousands of trees in this vicinity.

After you go south perhaps about a mile, you're getting up where you can start seeing the beautiful views of Jackson Hole. Out in front about a mile and a half directly to the east, you'll see Timbered Island, which is remnants of a glacial moraine that came down during the ice age when the Tetons were being carved by the glaciers. This part of the trail is just north of Burned Wagon Gulch, which has it's name from the early days when a wagon caught fire and burned there when they were getting out logs. The trail actually goes almost straight west for about a mile right on top of a lateral moraine. This is timbered all the way and you'll see some beautiful lodgepole pine as well as some Douglas Fir and Alpine Fir.

After going up this moraine for about a mile, you'll come to a well-signed trail junction and in going on up to Surprise Lake, you'll keep the right hand trail. The left hand trail goes pretty much on the level towards the south to Bradley Lake. (It's well to remember this cut off because sometimes people come down

Backpacking the Heights, Jackson Hole News photo.

late at night and are tired and not very observant and they have been known to think this is just another switch back and instead of going on down the moraine towards Lupine Meadows, they turn on this trail and it takes them over towards Bradley Lake. This can be very disturbing when they find that they have walked a mile or so on the wrong trail.) The trail that goes to the right starts a series of approximately 13 switch backs that go almost directly west, back and forth through the timber and openings on the side of the mountain. As one goes up the mountain, one can see some perpendicular gullys with no timber in them stretching practically all the way to the valley. (It might be interesting to note that the reason there is no timber in these gullys is the fact that these are avalanche gulches where the avalanches run nearly every year.) Any timber that starts to grow here has never gotten very high because it is swept away by periodic avalanches.

The junction with the Bradley Lake Trail (sometimes called the Valley Trail) is 7,260 feet in elevation. That means you have climbed a little over 500 feet and when you get there you can then judge your chances of making a comfortable hike all the way to the top. You've only come 500 feet and you have approximately 2,500 feet more to go. That is enough to discourage some people. You can make a decision whether to go slowly on up the trail, enjoying the marvelous views from those switch backs and the beautiful flowers and trees along the way and looking down on the lakes below and the Snake River and the panorama of Jackson Hole, or force yourself to go all the way up and becoming exhausted.

After leaving the Bradley Lake Trail and making two switch backs, at the end of the third switch back one will come to the remnants of an old trail that I more or less wore taking my climber's towards the Grand Teton in the early days before the main trail was built. This trail is still worn enough so it can be followed into Garnet Canyon, but before taking this faint trail through rather rough rocky ground which doesn't necessitate any climbing and is quite safe for the average hiker, one should make sure that one is allowed to do this by the Park Service because sometimes these old trails are closed. (Park Service note: This trail is signed "closed" although it is still used illegally.)

Going on, after another long switch back towards the north and then far south, one comes upon the junction of the regular trail that goes into Garnet Canyon at 8,400 feet elevation. (In the early days we called this Bradley Canyon and it is still known to some of the local folks as Bradley Canyon.) This was also built by the CCC's who had one of their main camps in a place called Moose Meadows, a little valley at the bottom of Garnet Canyon. More about this trail later.

Our trail turns off to the right and continues the switch backs. Along here one sees marvelous views of Jackson Hole, the various lakes, the highways down below, the cars crawling along on the various roads, the Snake River, and one has a very good view of the Gros Ventre Slide which is up where the Gros Ventre River enters the Gros Ventre mountains. (This slide is always of great interest to me because I happened to be in Jackson Hole at the time the slide went into the valley and made a lake several miles long. I was also in Jackson Hole at the time the dam broke and swept away the trees, ranches, cattle, machinery, bridges, and everything along the Gros Ventre River as far down as the Snake River.)

Surprise Lake is a bit of a surprise when one comes up on the trail. One does not expect to find this lake, which is in sort of a hollowed out place between two very steep canyon walls which go down on the north towards Glacier Gulch and to the south towards Garnet Canyon. The trail goes on past Surprise Lake up to Amphitheater Lake. (It might be interesting to note that the first time I climbed the Grand Teton in 1924, we climbed the Grand Teton from Delta Lake which is in Glacier Gulch to the north. Being inexperienced and a very foolish young boy at that time, after climbing the Grand Teton I found out that we could not go back that way because of the danger of deep snow. We came down in the afternoon, down what was then called Bradley Canyon and climbed the cliffs back up in the late afternoon, trying to get back to Delta Lake. Actually after climbing these cliffs, we just practically stuck our hands over the top of the cliff and here was this lake just a few feet away. It was a great surprise to us and we called it Surprise Lake. That was in July of 1924 when practically none of the higher lakes or the mountains in the Tetons were named.)

There is no trail up Glacier Gulch, but for people who are strong and are used to hiking off the trail, Glacier Gulch is one of the best off-trail hikes in the Tetons. There's a series of glaciated little cliffs, but one can work his way around them and it's a beautiful, beautiful climb. Sometimes it is necessary to use the hands for balance on some of the cliffs but one can walk all the way up to Delta Lake. We named it in 1924 because at the upper end it has quite a delta. The lake has filled up a great deal since 1924 from the glacial silt which is ground up rock carried down from the Teton Glacier by water through the moraine to the lake. Glacier Gulch is "off-trail" hiking and registration is required at Jenny Lake Ranger Station.

Due to heavy use in the past, camping is not permitted at Amphitheater Lake or near the shore of Surprise Lake. There are several good campsites a short distance from Surprise Lake to the east and north, some near the ridge overlooking Delta Lake.

When we first discovered and named Surprise Lake in 1924, we made our way down the cliffs (rather a precarious climb) to Delta Lake. Later on we discovered another route from Amphitheater Lake across to Teton Glacier, because if one goes down to Delta Lake, then one loses a lot of altitude and has to climb back up to Teton Glacier. The trail that was built by the CCC ends at Amphitheater Lake at the elevation of 9,698 feet. In 1925, I discovered a way of getting over to Teton Glacier without losing much altitude. That route goes almost directly north and a little bit west, up about a hundred feet in elevation from Amphitheater Lake and over a little pass. Then it drops down a rather steep slope for a few feet where one hits an outward sloping rock ledge where one can traverse to a flatter place at the foot of a very long snow slope that goes along the south side of the Grand Teton. Then you go across the bottom part of this snow slope which in the summer is not steep enough to be dangerous, but is certainly very slippery unless one has mountaineering shoes with cleats on them. As a matter of fact, anyone who is going up there and intends to climb the glacier should not go in tennis shoes, slick rubber, or leather soled shoes. An ice axe and crampons are recommended early in the season.

In the early days it took a great deal of balance and some danger to get around this ledge, especially with a pack. Several years later the Park Service put in a cable on the most dangerous place where people can hang on and make the passage more safely. One must remember that after one leaves Amphitheater Lake there is no longer a trail. There's perhaps a faint trail where other people have gone, but there are boulders to go over, scree slopes, slick rocks, and slick snow. When one crosses the first snow field, it's necessary to go up a very steep moraine which is the terminal moraine of the Teton Glacier. There the rocks are very apt to roll and the scree slopes may slide with each step. One should go over very close to the base of the cliff of the middle Teton Glacier and one can probably see where other people have traversed there. If one goes on the bottom part of the glacier, there will be some crevasses that the unwary could fall into, but it's worth going out on the glacier, especially if last year's snow has melted off.

If one goes up there early in the spring and the snow from the previous winter is still on top of the glacier, one is perhaps advised not to go out on this glacier un-roped because there are crevasses. If one goes out on the glacier perhaps a quarter of a mile and turns slightly up the glacier to the west, one can see the awe inspiring perpendicular north face of the Grand Teton which rises for the first thousand or so feet above the glacier. Also, one can look to the right, to the north and a little bit west, and see the snow fields of Mt. Owen. To the northeast one can see the spires of Teewinot which is a mountain which shows up so conspicuously from Jenny Lake. Many people think it is the Grand Teton, looking at it from Jenny Lake where the Grand Teton is not visible and is hidden by Teewinot. If one is adventursome and has good shoes and warm clothing, one might venture on up the glaciers to where there's an ice fall and some of the huge crevasses have opened up. Here I warn beginners who know nothing about glaciers to proceed with great caution, if at all, if they don't have any experience in mountaineering. (Park Service note: Climbing registration is required for anyone hiking in the vicinity of this glacier.)

It might be noted that the north face of the Grand Teton

which one sees directly above the glacier was first climbed by my brother Eldon and myself and one of my guides Jack Durrance in 1936. This was one of the first real acrobatic climbs made in America. Perhaps now it is a little bit overshadowed by some of the terrific perpendicular climbs they do in Yosemite, but at that time it was one of the most difficult climbs made in the United States. Leaving Amphitheater Lake about 3:00 a.m., we were on top of the Grand Teton at 7:00 p.m. that night. Then we came down the regular route which we knew very well to a camp that we had left at the head of Garnet Canyon.

There is a route for experienced hikers and people who are used to hiking over quite rough country to go from Surprise Lake down to the trail in Garnet Canyon. This traverse which is not a trail starts exactly where the outlet of Surprise Lake goes over the cliff and sprinkles down the cliffs into Garnet Canyon. This is a very, very steep slope with a lot of scree, a lot of loose rocks, and where small rocks, sand, and gravel will slide with a person. Of course, with a group of inexperienced people, this can be very dangerous. Unless one knows the techniques of descending in groups, the people above can dislodge large rocks which could severely injure the people below. So here again, this should only be done by people who are used to cross-country hiking and have been on rock slopes, scree slopes, and boulder slopes.

GARNET CANYON TRAIL

USGS Maps: Moose, Grand Teton
Distances: Lupine Meadows to Garnet Canyon Trail 3 miles,
E.R. 6.3 miles.
Trail end 4.1 miles, E.R. 8.6 miles.
The Platforms 4.2 miles, E.R. 8.8 miles.
The Meadows 4.8 miles, E.R. 10.3 miles.
Lower Saddle 6.3 miles, E.R. 16.3 miles.

The trail into Garnet Canyon is recommended for people who would like to get high up in the mountains but who would like a less exhausting way than going all the way up to Amphitheater and Surprise Lakes. If you plan to continue on up the canyon past the end of the trail, you must register for an "off-trail" hike at the Jenny Lake Ranger Station. The Garnet Canyon Trail starts at Lupine Meadows and is the same description as we have given for Amphitheater Lake Trail up to where the Garnet Canyon Trail takes off at an elevation of 8,400 feet.

As one gets into Garnet Canyon, if one looks carefully, one can see the remnants of an old trail that takes off to the left zig zagging downwards to the place we call Moose Meadows. If one goes down there to camp, there are some flat platforms that were built for the cook houses and the sleeping quarters of the spike camp of the CCC's, put there while they were building the main trail.

Moose Meadows is of some interest because I scouted a route from Jenny Lake to Moose Meadows. In 1924, after I'd first climbed the Grand Teton, Mr. Owen who was in Jackson at that time who had made the first ascent of the Grand in 1898, wanted to try to climb the mountain again. A group in Jackson was organized to make the climb with him. They wanted to go as far as they could on horses. Before that trip started, I made two or three foot trips and found a way to bring the horses. I went ahead of the horses by foot and led them through a labyrinth of cliffs and downed timber and gullys and we got the whole pack outfit into Moose Meadows. This was certainly the first time that horses had been brought in to Garnet Canyon. Moose Meadows was as far as horses could go in those days before the CCC's built the trail into Moose Meadows. Also, it might be interesting to note to a person going on up to the end of the trail, that to the south up on top of the cliffs near the end of the trail was where the Billy Owen party brought their horses in 1898. They left the horses up on the cliff and came down the cliffs into Garnet Canyon. They proceeded on up Garnet Canyon to the lower saddle from where they made their first successful climb of the Grand Teton.

The upper end of the trail in Garnet Canyon is where one finds the last trees in the canyon. Where the trail ends, if one crosses the creek and goes up 40 or 50 feet in elevation to the south, one will find a platform where there are some trees. This area is now called the Platforms. This is one of the places where I established one of my first climbing camps in the 1920's. This was before the trail was built into the canyon and was one of the last places where we could find wood to camp. Now days climbers have also used this place to a great extent and have worn down some of the perennial plants so it is advised that people not camp there unless it's an emergency.

Going on up Garnet Canyon from the Platforms, is not difficult at all. One can proceed and go clear to the base of Middle Teton. The route from the Platforms on up the canyon stays pretty much along the stream and takes a little balancing over and under and around large rocks as you proceed upward, but there is no climbing as such involved in this upper end of the route. Anyone with good shoes and average balance can safely go on up the canyon. There is a foot path going up through this area which is worn out by the hikers and climbers, but it is not a maintained trail.

The upper end of the canyon below the base of Middle Teton is an area now called the Meadows where there are large open flat places where people may camp. To the right and above the Meadows, one can see the top of the Grand Teton and directly in front of you as you face the Grand Teton and between the Grand Teton and the Meadows there are some beautiful falls coming down off the cliffs. These are called the Spalding Falls in honor of Reverend Spalding who was with Mr. Owen on his first ascent of the Grand Teton in 1898.

Pine Martin, Jackson Hole News photo.

Most climbers take the trail to the right to go up to the lower saddle. However, for most people it is quite difficult getting up the beginning of this trail where it goes up to below Spalding Falls. This trail is very steep and has loose dirt and rocks and great care should be exercised in climbing through this area. The trail leads upward and over near the falls and then traverses on up above the falls and passes a place commonly known as the Petzoldt Caves. This is a place underneath some big boulders that I dug out in the 1920's where we used to camp to get out of the rain in preparation for climbing the Grand Teton. It was from this bivouac underneath these boulders that the first winter climb of the Grand Teton was made. This climb was done by my brother Eldon Petzoldt and a native by the name of Fred Brown and myself in 1936.

The Spalding Falls area would probably be as far as a hiker in very good shape would want to reach and return in the same day to Jenny Lake. However, if a hiker is in very good condition and wishes to push himself and not take the time to enjoy the country, he could go further on up and either proceed up the canyon to the left or to the right of Middle Teton and go higher. But in this area for the most part of the year one would get into very steep and loose rock country or steep snow fields. Unless a person carries an ice ax and knows how to use it and is experienced enough to know the dangers, one is not advised to go beyond the Meadows.

Climbers who want to climb the Grand Teton can proceed in several ways. If they are strong and in good condition and have permission, they can camp down as far as Moose Meadows. I have made the Grand Teton many, many times up to the top from Moose Meadows and back, although it's a long day and it takes a person in very, very good condition to make it. Camping in the Meadows below Spalding Falls or at the Platforms or places in between is practical. Here again, campers need to be very careful of the country and camp without digging any trenches or disturbing the soil in any way.

While in this canyon, when one has to relieve one's self, one should go as far away from the stream as possible among the large boulders so that any pollution would be well filtered before it gets back into the stream. All human debris should certainly be buried. One going into the canyon for an overnight stay should carry a shovel and dig slit trenches and then carefully cover them after use. This should be as far away from the water as possible.

Some people like to go on up the canyon above the Meadows and above the caves and camp on the Middle Teton Glacier or the moraine close by or even up on the lower saddle. Just below the saddle in the moraine, there are a few places that have been scraped out and flattened just large enough to pitch a small tent. Some climbers use this area as a base camp to climb the Grand.

Very, very experienced people for most of the year can go all the way to the saddle following the snow fields that lay along the base of the Middle Grand. Other people may wish to follow the slight trail that goes along the top of the moraine to the base of the cliff below the lower saddle. There at this cliff near a small waterfall, one may find a fixed rope left there by the guides which will allow them to go up a very precipitous cliff for 50 or 75 feet. There they will reach narrow trails that zig zag on up and over the saddle. People carrying packs should be warned that even with a rope this climb is very, very difficult.

The quansit hut up on the lower saddle between the Middle and the Grand Teton was donated by a man named Mr. Smith who once was a client of the American school of Mountaineering when I had it in conjunction with Ben Exum. The guides carried the quansit hut up to the saddle and put it up. Generally it has been reserved for the use of the guides where they can leave some of their equipment. The quansit hut is still used in some rescue operations and some rescue equipment is stored there during the winter.

From the saddle one has some of the outstanding views in the Tetons. One can see not only all the way across to Jackson Hole, the Gros Ventre, the Absorakas and part of the Wind River range, but one can also look over into Idaho and see Pierre's Hole which is commonly known as the Teton Basin and over the great Snake River Drainage and the large spread of the irrigated potato farms. One can even see to the Great Buttes of the Craters of the Moon area where the terrific lava beds are. Just north of that, one can make out where the terrific experimentation is being done by the Atomic Energy Commission. One can also look further on over into the Sawtooth Range and see Mt. Hayden and the mountains around the ski area near Ketchum and Hayley, Idaho. One can also see hundreds of miles into the Yellowstone country to the north and even into the Bitterroot Mountains in Montana.

From the saddle very, very experienced hikers and mountaineers can descend on the Idaho side of the saddle into the south fork of Cascade Canyon and make their way downward around the mountains and come out at Jenny Lake. One cannot go directly off the lower part of the saddle to the west because the terrain drops off in a nearly perpendicular wall onto a glacier below. The route goes up the saddle to the Black Dike which crosses the saddle to the north which is probably two or three hundred feet above you and a quarter of a mile away. From this Black Dike going down to the left, a very experienced mountaineer can make his way down a very steep scree slope or very steep snow slopes depending upon the time of year and get into the valley on the west side of the saddle. From this valley just below the saddle, one can make his way on down to the south fork of Cascade Canyon where he will reach a trail which goes on down the canyon to come out at Jenny Lake. This same trail which one finds in the south fork of Cascade Canyon also goes to the left on up the canyon, crosses over the divide behind all of the Tetons and goes clear around and comes out on the Phillips Pass Trail above Wilson on highway 22 west of Jackson.

From the Meadows, one can go up the branch of Garnet Canyon to the left, between Middle and South Teton where there are many lesser peaks to be climbed from that area. If one goes up to the saddle between the Middle and the South Tetons, it is extremely difficult to get down to the vicinity of Ice Flow Lake below. If one looks at the Topog maps, one will see that there is a very precipitous area immediately below the saddle between you and the lakes. However, one can climb up around to the west of South Teton and descend along the ridge to the same level as the lake and then swing around to Ice Flow Lake if he wishes. Near the lower part of this western ridge below South Teton, one would again reach the trail that comes up

South Cascade Canyon. Also, near where one reaches the upper end of this south fork Cascade Canyon trail near the lower part of this ridge coming off of South Teton, one can proceed almost due west and cross through the wall at this point and proceed on directly over to Sunset Lake where he will encounter the Teton Crest Trail in Alaska Basin. This sort of "off-trail" hike is only for experienced mountaineers with permission from the rangers.

It might be interesting to note that in 1924, I brought horses up Death Canyon and around into the Ice Flow Lake area and camped there, which was quite a feat for horses in those days. I made a trip with Mr. Owens to the top of Grand Teton and back in one day from this camp. This was to celebrate his 64th birthday and we did the one day trip on that day. This took place 26 years after he made the first ascent of the Grand Teton.

Tops of the Tetons, Jackson Hole News photo by Virginia Huidekoper

Teton Park Center

72

BRADLEY LAKE TRAIL

USGS Maps: Moose, Grand Teton
Distances: Bradley Lake 2 miles, E.R. 3 miles.

The Bradley Lake Trail which also includes the Taggart Lake Trail starts about three miles north of the park headquarters at Moose and about a mile from the old park headquarters on Beaver Creek. Cars can be left at the Taggart Lake Trail parking area which is a turnaround on the west side of the road just before you cross Taggart Creek. This is not a real difficult hike and for those who want to make a nice easy all day trip, this is what it should be. The trip could be done in an afternoon, but it's a nice kind of a slow hike for folks that want to start out in the cool of the morning and take their lunch and spend the day enjoying the scenery around the lakes and looking up at the tall peaks directly above the lakes. One can take off on the trail at the parking area and go directly west where in a quarter of a mile he'll hit the junction of the Beaver Creek Trail and the trail going up Taggart Creek.

The trail generally follows along the north side of Taggart Creek and then after about three quarters of a mile it forks, the left fork going to Taggart Lake and the right fork leading on over to Bradley Lake. This is a good trail and plainly marked. Along the sides of this trail one can see the terrific impact of the down draft storms that along here and other places have completely flattened some areas in the forest. Many of these trees fell across the trail during this storm but have all been cut out and the trail is now clear of any obstructions.

If one continues on past the trail junction on the Bradley Lake Trail, one soon climbs up onto the huge moraine which separates Bradley and Taggart Lakes since both of these lakes were gouged out by ancient glaciers which came down Garnet Canyon and Avalanche Canyon. Huge glacial moraines were deposited in between and below the two lakes. The high moraine between the two lakes is a lateral moraine which was forced up by the sides of the glaciers which gouged out these two lakes. The Bradley Lake Trail goes to the top of the moraine then turns and heads off towards the north and switchbacks as it descends the 100 feet or so as it reaches the level of the lake.

After traversing the east shore of Bradley Lake, you will cross a manmade bridge and continue on to the northwest and climb up over another moraine which would be the lateral moraine on the north side of Garnet Canyon. The trail proceeds upwards where in about a mile and a half it joins the trail from Lupine Meadows which goes up to Surprise and Amphitheater Lakes and also swings into Garnet Canyon. This trail running from Bradley Lake up over the moraine to join the trail going to Surprise Lake and Garnet Canyon, is not one of the more heavily used trails in this area, but that in itself would make a nice day's hike for one coming out of Lupine Meadows and going up the Surprise Lake Trail, over to Bradley Lake, and back to the Cottonwood Creek turnout or the Taggart Lake parking area to be met there by someone with an automobile.

Such of Nature's works are always worthy of our preservation and protection; and\the further we become separated. . .from that pristine wildness and beauty, the more pleasure does the mind of enlightened man feel in recurring to those scenes, when he can have them preserved for his eyes and his mind to dwell upon.

—George Catlin

TAGGART LAKE TRAIL

USGS Maps: Moose, Grand Teton
Distances: Taggart Lake 1.6 miles, E.R. 2.2 miles.

The Taggart Lake Trail also takes off at the same place as the Bradley Lake Trail from the Taggart Lake Trail parking area. About a mile up this trail at the trail junction of the Bradley Lake-Taggart Lake Trail, you would turn left and go down through the trees along the edge of the moraine to reach the edge of Taggart Lake. When you reach the edge of the lake you will come into another trail which traverses around the east end of Taggart Lake. This trail proceeds around to the north end and climbs up the moraine between the two lakes and joins the Bradley Lake Trail over near the shore of Bradley Lake.

Where the Taggart Lake Trail first joins the trail going around Taggart Lake, one can also turn to the left and cross the outlet of Taggart Lake on a man-made bridge and continue south through the timber over to Beaver Creek. Here on the creek one will reach another trail junction where by taking the left fork, one can go down the Beaver Creek Trail which will return you to the Taggart Lake Trail parking area from where you started.

The loop trails going to and around Bradley and Taggart Lakes are very interesting from the standpoint of timber and flowers and of getting good views of the mountains and the lakes. Most of the time one is in the wooded area and not too high above the valley. Consequently, your views of the valley and the Gros Ventre Range and up towards Yellowstone are limited in this easterly direction. One does not get high enough to get good views of the valley but you do have very good views of the high mountain peaks above the lakes.

DEATH CANYON TRAIL

USGS Maps: Grand Teton, Mount Bannon
Distances: Patrol Cabin 3.7 miles, E.R. 5.7 miles.
Fox Creek Pass 9.2 miles, E.R. 14.8 miles.
Alaska Basin via Fox Creek Pass 14.9 miles, E.R. 20.5 miles.
Alaska Basin via Alaska Basin Trail 9 miles, E.R. 17 miles.

Going part way up Death Canyon and returning the same day can be a very beautiful trip. Death Canyon with its terrifically steep walls and its view back towards Jackson Lake are well worth the day hike. This hike would generally start by going to the park headquarters at Moose. From here you drive southwest on the Wilson Road approximately three miles to where a road turns off sharply to the right just after crossing Stewart Creek. Turning right up this road, one would drive towards the White Grass Dude Ranch but take a left fork as you near the ranch and drive up to the old White Grass Ranger Station. This station was originally an old Forest Service Ranger Station before the park service took over the area. Those planning an overnight or "off-trail" hike should get a permit at the Moose Ranger Station.

The trail goes to the northwest beyond the end of the road where in a few hundred yards one hits the old Valley Trail traversing around the base of the mountains in this area. Turning left on this Valley Trail, one proceeds gradually over and above Phelps Lake where, at another trail junction, you turn right and proceed up Death Canyon. For about a mile from this trail junction, you will start climbing fairly rapidly and then you'll go up steeply to where you reach an old patrol cabin. Near this cabin the trail branches. The right fork heads up the Alaska Basin Trail going up to the summit and over into Alaska Basin.

Starting from an elevation at around 6,800 feet at White Grass Ranger Station, it would be an extremely ambitious person who wanted to climb clear up into Alaska Basin, where the divide going into it is approximately 10,500 feet or a climb of around 4,000 feet, and do all this in one day and return that same day. A nice day's hike would be going up the canyon about four miles to the patrol cabin and returning.

ALASKA BASIN TRAIL

At this patrol cabin junction on the Death Canyon Trail, a manmade trail, which was made by the CCC's in the early days, takes off towards the north. This is a very precipitous trail going up in a series of zig zags that goes up towards Static Peak and along the base of Buck Mountain towards the north. As this trail climbs upward, it leaves the last timber at about 9,600 feet elevation and from there it will continue along above timberline to a height of approximately 10,800 feet. Then it will continue in a northwesterly direction, traversing and dropping gradually as it goes into the divide above Alaska Basin. This divide separates the drainages where on one side the Death Canyon drainage runs down into the South Fork of the Snake River towards the east. On the other side of the drainage, the water runs down into the south fork of Teton Creek which drains into Pierre's Hole and the north fork of the Snake River.

Dropping into Alaska Basin one will get into a beautiful, beautiful valley which is a high plateau country that we named Alaska Basin on our trip in there with horses in 1924, because of its terrific snow slopes and vast expanses of snow and mountains.

DEATH CANYON TRAIL

When I first took horses up through here in 1924, the trail that we just described up on the side of Buck Mountain was not there. The old trail that we took went on up Death Canyon above the present patrol cabin and was a very, very rough trail in the old days. This trail was made by the early sheep men and miners and other people wanting to go from Jackson to cross into Idaho. This trail continues on up Death Canyon Creek and now is a good trail and a very, very interesting one. It continues on up a long ways through this beautiful, beautiful canyon. The trail goes through a country of grassy land and meadows and scattered pine forests, with cliffs above you on all sides and with marvelous views.

From above the patrol cabin at about 8,000 feet, the trail climbs very gradually for about six miles to the upper end of Death Canyon. At about the 8,600 foot elevation, one begins to climb more rapidly and the trail becomes very steep as you approach Fox Creek Pass at the high point of the trail at 9,600 feet where you will join the Teton Crest Trail.

Turning right, you will proceed out onto the Death Canyon Shelf. This shelf has perpendicular cliffs below and above it. This narrow grassy ledge, with the high cliffs above and the steep precipitous cliffs below, is where I first rode horses over in 1924 on our way to Ice Flow Lake to climb the west side of the Grand Teton. This beautiful section of the trail along the shelf runs for about 4 miles towards the north and gradually east where you'll pass through the Mt. Meek Pass just to the right of Mt. Meek.

The Mt. Meek Pass is at 9,726 feet so one can see that this past 4 miles along the shelf, one gained only an altitude of maybe 126 feet. It is a most beautiful, beautiful trail with the most miraculous views down Death Canyon below. From the trail you look down into the steep cliffs below and at all of the mountains around, towards the north and the south and the view of Jackson Hole towards the east. This results in a most pleasant hike along this ledge.

Going on over the divide at Mt. Meek's Pass following along what is called the Teton Crest Trail, one comes to a very steep zig zag section which is called the Sheep Steps. In 1924 when we took horses down this very, very steep precipitous trail, it was extremely difficult. These switch backs were made by the early sheepherders bringing their sheep in and out of Alaska Basin and one cannot ride down on a horse. One has to walk and lead the horse through this dangerous section. This trail was reconstructed by the Forest Service and except for lingering snow due to northern exposure, is in good condition. Most people coming into Alaska Basin take the Alaska Basin Trail described earlier, which comes up from the patrol cabin, because it is such a short cut into the basin.

Canyon Hiking, Jackson Hole News photo by G. Bellerose

OPEN CANYON TRAIL

USGS Maps: Grand Teton, Teton Village, Rendezvous Peak
Distances: Mt. Hunt Divide 7.3 miles, E.R. 13.1 miles.
　　　　　　Granite Canyon Trail 11.4 miles, E.R. 17.2 miles.

The Open Canyon Trail begins back on the Death Canyon
Trail which had its beginning at the White Grass Ranger
Station near the White Grass Ranch about a mile and a half off
the road and three miles south of the Moose Ranger Station.

Going west from the White Grass Ranger Station for about a
mile and a half, you'll reach a trail junction where the Valley
Trail takes off to the left and goes around the upper side of
Phelps Lake. When you leave the Death Canyon Trail, the trail
starts south where in about a quarter of a mile you'll cross
Death Canyon Creek about a third of a mile above where it
enters Phelps Lake. Continuing south along this trail for about
three quarters of a mile you'll reach another trail junction. Turn
to the right and you'll enter the lower part of Open Canyon.

This trail going up Open Canyon is a nice trail and goes over
into Granite Canyon to join the North Granite Creek Trail
about a mile and a half below the Teton Crest Trail. It proceeds
up Open Canyon staying above the stream and in gradual
switch backs gains altitude fairly rapidly. After about three
miles, the trail leaves Open Canyon and turns south to climb
steeply for about a half mile to the Mt. Hunt Divide. Then it
proceeds on around the east side of Mt. Hunt. From this divide,
you traverse and lose a little altitude, going around the south
slopes of Mt. Hunt. In about three miles you will hit the Granite
Canyon Trail in the north fork of Granite Creek. These
combined trails then go on up towards the north and west up
Granite Creek where in about a mile and a half they join the
Teton Crest Trail. Turning to the right on this trail about three
miles will bring you to Fox Creek Pass above Death Canyon or
turning to the left on the Teton Crest Trail about two and a half
miles brings you to another divide above the middle fork, where
you'll cross over into the upper reaches of Moose Creek.

GRANITE CANYON TRAIL

USGS Maps: Teton Village, Rendezvous Peak
Distances: Upper Patrol Cabin 6.3 miles, E.R. 9.6 miles.
          Open Canyon Trail 7 miles, E.R. 11.1 miles.
          Teton Crest Trail 8.2 miles, E.R. 13.3 miles.
          Marion Lake 8.8 miles, E.R. 14.5 miles.

This is one of the prettiest canyons in the Tetons with the trail going through a combination of forests, beautiful open meadows and with scenic cliffs bordering on both sides. A variety of loop trails are possible. Coming out Open Canyon is about nineteen miles. Coming back Death Canyon is about 24 miles. Starting on Rendezvous Mountain Trail at the top of the tram is about twelve miles.

This is a well marked and maintained trail starting at the signed trailhead on the Moose-Wilson Road. It's about two miles along the road from Teton Village or about six miles from Moose. If you're staying in the Moose area you'll drive down from there. If you're staying at Jackson it's closer going towards Wilson and taking the Moose-Wilson road past Teton Village to the trailhead. It's a good road with part of it being gravel.

At the trailhead there is a good sign giving distances to ten choices of places to reach by using this trail. There is a place to park which will accommodate about thirty cars.

It's a mile and a half of pretty flat hiking to the entrance of the canyon, where there is a patrol cabin and you'll cross the Valley Trail which runs along the base of the range. Going up the canyon you climb gradually, following the stream all the way to the top where you'll join the Skyline Trail in a little over eight miles. Turn right on this trail and you're a little over a half mile from Marion Lake. For a variation on the return trip, you could go south along the Teton Crest Trail to the Middle Fork Cut Off Trail. Take this across to join the Rendezvous Mountain Trail and go down it to Granite Creek and then back to your car.

RENDEZVOUS MOUNTAIN TRAIL

USGS Maps: Teton Village, Rendezvous Peak.
Distances: Top to Teton Village 12 miles, E.R. 12 miles.

This trail is a highly scenic one, giving you a little of almost every kind of view available in the Tetons. A big attraction is that it's easy to hike, as it starts at the top of the Aerial Tramway which runs from Teton Village to the ridge of Rendezvous Mountain. The trail is about twelve miles long and you can come out at Teton Village or on the Moose-Wilson road at the Granite Canyon Trailhead. Also this trail will connect you with the Teton Crest Trail from which you can go in either direction, connecting to numerous trails coming up all the canyons along the Teton Range.

It should be emphasized that this trial, though all down hill, is a very long one day hike. A person should be prepared physically and also take proper equipment. He should have good boots, extra clothing and a lunch in his day pack. The weather can change very quickly from a nice warm day to a very cold rainy one. Also one should start early if he wants to get back in the daylight. One thing on the plus side, you don't have to carry any water as there is plenty all along the route.

The tram runs all summer from Memorial Day usually to the end of September. The ride begins at the base of the clock tower in Teton Village. There is plenty of parking space nearby. The tickets cost $3.50 for adults and takes you up four thousand feet.

From the top of the tram, you go along the ridge to the west on a trail that is part of a Nature Interpretive trail. Then you'll come to a prominent saddle where you'll turn to the north and enter the Teton National Park. There are signs here.

From the saddle it heads generally northeast to a little switch back and on through the timber. Then it breaks out into the head of an open bowl above one of the tributaries of Granite Creek. Soon it climbs a bit for about a half mile around a ridge. Then it drops gradually back to the west through occasional open meadows to cross the South Fork of Granite Creek. Another half mile of easy hiking brings you to a trail junction where the Middle Fork Cut Off Trail comes in. This trail runs across to join the Teton Crest Trail, less than a mile to the west.

The Rendezvous Mountain Trail continues down a prominent open area where in about a mile and a half you'll cross Granite Creek on a bridge and join the Granite Canyon Trail on the other side. Nearby is a patrol cabin where a Wilderness Ranger is stationed by the Park Service in the summer. It is a small square log cabin, built probably in the early thirties.

Coming down Granite Canyon you follow the stream all the way. It is a pretty canyon, with timber and open meadows and towering cliffs on both sides most of the way. In about five miles you'll reach the Valley Trail near another patrol cabin. From here it's a mile and a half to the Granite Canyon trailhead or about two miles along the Valley Trail to Teton Village.

Columbines, Bridger-Teton National Forest photo by W. N. Jacks

AVALANCHE CANYON ROUTE

USGS Maps: Moose, Grand Teton
Distances: Lake Taminah 5 miles, E.R. 9.8 miles.
          Snowdrift Lake 6 miles, E.R. 12.7 miles.

This cross-country hike is for those who prefer something a little bit out of the ordinary and want to go into what I think might be the most beautiful part of the Grand Teton National Park as well as the most isolated section in the park. This trip is for people with good foot gear and warm clothing and with much experience in finding their way through the mountains with the use of quad maps. One could possible make the trip up into Avalanche Canyon and back in one day, but this would be the ultimate in camping experience in the Tetons if one could get permission to stay overnight up in this area. At this writing there are very few people that ever go up there. By very careful selection of routes one can go through the boulder fields and over patches of snow and around cliffs and work themselves up the game trails into the top of the canyon. I am certainly firm in my belief that this is one of the most beautiful and rewarding hikes in the entire United States.

Take the Bradley Lake Trail beginning at the Taggart Lake Trail turnaround and go around the south side of Taggart Lake. There, one leaves the trail and, making ones own way through the trees towards the west around the lake, one begins to work his way up through the trees. Following game trails heading up Taggart Creek, one proceeds into Avalanche Canyon.

There is some semblance of trails in this canyon and I believe people have had horses up there, but there are no trails on the maps. After one gets out of the timber and brush near Taggart Lakes, it is not a horrendous trip for those who have had some experience hiking cross country through areas which have no trails. There is a worn route nearly to the forks but beyond there you find your own way. Taggart Creek itself forks and the south fork goes towards the south towards Static Peak and the lower reaches of Buck Mountain. The main Taggart Creek proceeds west from where the two parts come together and

Avalanche Divide, Jackson Hole News photo by G. Bellerose

goes up to some very beautiful falls called Shoshoko Falls. Here by very careful route picking, one can get around some very precipitous glaciated cliffs and boulder fields, and then go around Lake Taminah. From there, proceed west on up to Snowdrift Lake which is at an elevation of about 10,000 feet. This whole area above where the creek forks is all above timberline, amid beautiful peaks towering high on all sides.

Hikers going up to this country, and up any of the side canyons above here should know snow techniques and have the proper equipment to handle the steep snow slopes. One can traverse north and a little bit west from Snowdrift Lake and go on to the ridge that runs down west of South Teton Peak and near the bottom of this ridge pass through a divide. Here, one may turn to the left and cross over the wall where there's a route down to Sunset Lake. Also, it would be possible to go up this ridge towards the east and climb the South Teton, or make one's way around the South Teton into the divide separating South Teton from Middle Teton and go back down Garnet Canyon.

It was near this divide north of Snow Drift Lake where we brought our horses through from Sunset Lake back in 1924 with Mr. Owen to climb the west side of Grand Teton. We followed the Death Canyon Trail to its top where it joined the Teton Crest Trail, came along the Teton Crest through Mt. Meek Pass, down the Sheep's Steps and into Alaska Basin where we camped near Sunset Lake. From this lake we went up almost due east through a pass in the wall and traversed on almost a level plain over to Ice Flow Lake where we made our base camp. From here we went northeast up along the base of Middle Teton, traversing across the glacier in a northeasterly direction and worked our way up through the steep scree and snow slopes up above the saddle into the Black Dike. From there we climbed on up to the top of the Grand Teton.

HIDDEN FALLS TRAIL

USGS Maps: Jenny Lake, Moose.
Distances: Boat dock to Hidden Falls .5 mile, E.R. .9 mile.
          To Inspiration Point 1 mile, E.R. 1.9 miles.
          Lake outlet to Hidden Falls 2.5 miles, E.R. 2.9 miles.
          Lake outlet to Inspiration Point 3 miles, E.R. 3.9
          miles.

Perhaps one of the most popular trips in all of the Tetons is to take a boat from the boat landing near the outlet of Jenny Lake, where there is a large car parking area between Cottonwood Creek and the Jenny Lake Ranger Station, and go across the lake to the boat landing near where Cascade Creek comes out of the Cascade Canyon into Jenny Lake. From the boat landing a trail goes approximately half a mile and rises about 200 feet to a place where one can view Hidden Falls, which is a beautiful view and a very beautiful falls. If you continue on up the trail for another half mile, gaining approximately 250 feet in elevation, you'll come out at a place called Inspiration Point which is directly east of Hidden Falls. This is an overlook of Jenny Lake and the Jackson Hole area. This is a trip that one can do in a few hours and is a trip that many tourists could do who would not consider taking an all day hike or an overnight trip to the mountains. One can walk to Hidden Falls from the parking area or from the boat landing at the outlet of Jenny Lake on a well marked and well used trail that goes around Jenny Lake on the southwest side for approximately two miles. There the trail joins the one coming up from the boat landing and one can continue on up to Hidden Falls and Inspiration Point. Horses going across on the trail tie up below Hidden Falls. There are actually three ways that one can get to Hidden Falls; by boat, by walking and by hiring a horse. One can make a combination of any one of these by riding over and walking back or walking over and riding back, whichever they prefer. The horse concession is located near the south exit of Jenny Lake.

CASCADE CANYON TRAIL

USGS Maps: Jenny Lake, Mount Moran, Grand Teton
Distances: Trail Forks 6.5 miles, E.R. 8.6 miles.
          Lake Solitude 9.2 miles, E.R. 13.7 miles.
          Paintbrush Divide 11.6 miles, E.R. 19.5 miles.
          Hurricane Pass 11.6 miles, E.R. 18.8 miles.

The trail up Cascade Canyon is one of the most beautiful trail hikes in the Tetons. Unfortunately because of its accessability by boat and a good trail and because it is such a beautiful trail, it is one of the most heavily used in the Tetons. If one wants solitude and wants to get away from it all, one is advised not to take this trail. It is used to the maximum and is not restricted by the Park Service for day hikes. It is very advisable to check with them before ever going on this trail or those leading off from it because the rules and regulations may change from year to year in order that the Park Service can protect this country from over use and to conserve its eco-system and natural beauty. (Park Service note: The camping areas in Cascade Canyon are filled in advance in July and August. No camping is allowed below the forks or at Lake Solitude.)

The trail starts on the Hidden Falls trail. See that description for the beginning. After one passes the beautiful view of Hidden Falls and Inspiration Point, the trail follows up the canyon on the north side of the creek. It stays on the bottom for about four miles to where it reaches the first trail junction. There is no chance of getting lost or getting off this trail as it stays right along the bottom all the way. There is the roaring river on one side and the steep canyon walls up above you on each side. The scenery in this canyon is spectacular. The north slopes of Mt. Owen with a series of cliffs and snow steps is one of the most beautiful mountain scenes in the Tetons. Equally spectacular is the perpendicular sides of Teewinot which border the canyon on the south. On the north side, there are also great perpendicular cliffs which lead up to Symmetry Spire and Rock of Ages. This canyon has a particular interest to me as it was from here that I made the first ascent up the north side of Mt. Owen.

LAKE SOLITUDE TRAIL

When one reaches the forks of the trail after crossing the bridge over Cascade Creek, the right hand fork is called the Lake Solitude Trail. This trail goes for approximately three miles from the junction up to Lake Solitude. From here one gets one of the most spectacular and striking views of the Grand Teton. I doubt if any view of the Grand Teton surpasses the one from this location. This view has been popularized in many paintings and millions of photographs.

It is possible to go all the way from Jenny Lake to Lake Solitude and back in one day, but this should be done only by people in very good condition and people who wish to push at the expense of enjoying the beautiful scenery and the flora and fauna in route. Camping is restricted in this area and changes from year to year so one should check with the Park Service before making his plans for overnight trips. In camping anywhere in these mountains, one should be very careful to obey to the letter the spirit of conservation practices that we have briefly outlined previously.

PAINTBRUSH DIVIDE TRAIL

For the overnight camper who wishes to continue on a very adventuresome and beautiful hike, one can continue from Lake Solitude on up over the Paintbrush Divide Trail. This trail climbs very, very steeply for approximately 1,600 feet in about two miles of climbing. From the divide one then drops very swiftly down on the other side and approaches the very beautiful Holly Lake. One has come from above timberline down into scattered patches of timber in the Holly Lake area which is at an elevation of 9,400 feet. Early in the season this trail from Lake Solitude over to Holly Lake should be attempted only by very experienced mountaineers who have ice axes and know how to handle steep snow slopes. Later on in the summer, this trail becomes almost devoid of snow except in the high passes and can be travelled safely by the ordinary hiker. Here again the rangers should be consulted before attempting this high area in the early spring where there's possibilities of crossing steep hard packed snow.

SOUTH FORK CASCADE CANYON TRAIL

The south fork of Cascade Creek (where one takes the left hand fork at the junction at the top of Cascade Canyon, a few hundred yards above the bridge that crosses Cascade Creek) is a trail that goes along what is commonly called the Skyline Trail (part of the Teton Crest Trail) which is a popular trail for going all the way in back of the Tetons, through Alaska Basin, down Death Canyon to Phelps Lake and back to the White Grass Ranger Station. At the White Grass Ranger Station one could arrange to be picked up by automobile or he could hike along the Valley Trail clear back up past Bradley Lake and on to Jenny Lake from where he started.

The south fork of Cascade Canyon has a very well developed trail and here again one is getting into some terrific views of the Grand Teton and Mr. Owen from the west side. About three miles up this trail one begins to climb rapidly through the head waters of the south fork to where one reaches Hurricane Pass. Here, one can look over into Idaho to Pierre's Hole and across the Idaho valleys, the Snake River Valley, and the Sawtooth Mountains beyond. Looking back towards the east one again sees the magnificent peaks of the Tetons from the west side.

From about a mile below Hurricane Pass in the south fork of Cascade Canyon another little used trail takes off to the left and goes almost due south, climbing gradually up to another saddle overlooking Snow Drift Lake. From this little saddle several possibilities exist for the very experienced mountaineer. One could climb the South Teton from this point, going up the ridge directly to the east of him. Or one could swing around to the north into the south fork of Garnet Canyon and return back to Jenny Lake on the Garnet Canyon Trail. Another possibility would be to make your way down to Snow Drift Lake and then proceed on down Avalanche Canyon to Taggart Lake and from there return to Jenny Lake. Another possibility would be to turn towards the west from this higher divide and proceed down to Sunset Lake in Alaska Basin and explore that area for awhile. Then one could take the Alaska Basin Trail which crosses over into Death Canyon and comes out at the White Grass Ranger Station near Phelps Lake.

HANGING CANYON ROUTE

USGS Maps: Jenny Lake, Mount Moran.
Distances: Lake of the Crags 3 miles, E.R. 8.4 miles.

A beautiful off the trail one day hike or possibly over night camping trip can be made into Hanging Canyon on the west side of Jenny Lake. One could take a boat across the lake from the outlet, or hike from the outlet along the Valley Trail past Cascade Canyon (as one would go towards Hidden Falls) and continue along on the west shore of Jenny Lake possibly another quarter of a mile to where the Hanging Canyon stream enters Jenny Lake. Or one can approach Hanging Canyon which leads up to Rams Head Lake and Lake of the Craggs by taking the trail that starts near the Jenny Lake Lodge. From here, one would cross the bridge at the outlet of String Lake and then go south along the Valley Trail on the upper west side of Jenny Lake. Follow this trail until it reaches the bridge which crosses Hanging Canyon Creek.

There is no maintained trail up this canyon but hikers have worn a "path" of sorts up the rugged slopes as far as Ramshead Lake. Experienced hikers should be able to make their way along this route.

When one reaches the Lake of the Crags one will have climbed approximately 2,800 feet in about two miles of hiking. This means that you are going up very, very steep grassy slopes over steep rock faces where rope work is not necessary but where some bracing of the hands and balancing is required and good experience at route picking is essential.

Early in the season there can be some very, very steep snow slopes along here which should be avoided. If one has to travel over these steep slopes, the trip should be abandoned unless one is a mountaineer with the right experience and equipment for this type of hiking. Sometimes these snow slopes cover the stream and the unwary hiker may drop through the snow into the water where the heat of the water has melted the snow from underneath leaving narrow invisible bridges. This would be a very, very dangerous experience for the inexperienced hiker going near these snow covered streams. People have been

Lake of the Crags, Jackson Hole News photo by R. Murphy.

known to lose their lives by falling into these hidden places.

When you get up into the Lake of the Crags area, you are surrounded by small perpendicular peaks that are a beautiful miniature of the gigantic peaks found in other areas of the Tetons. Around you on all sides are these perpendicular spires and peaks and the area is studded with snow fields. This area has one of the most beautiful mountain views in the Tetons, lacking the grandeur of the spectacular great peaks but in many ways surpassing them all in beauty. This is a place that has always affected me as a sort of a Shangrila, where I like to sit and think and contemplate the solitude and beauties of nature.

*One day the sun shall shine more brightly than
ever he has done, shall perchance shine into our
minds and hearts, and light up our whole lives with
a great awakening light, as warm and serene
and golden as on a bankside in autumn.*

— Henry David Thoreau

Pika, Bridger-Teton National Forest photo.

PAINTBRUSH CANYON TRAIL

USGS Maps: Jenny Lake, Mount Moran.
Distances: Holly Lake 6.2 miles, E.R. 11.3 miles.
            Paintbrush Divide 7.9 miles, E.R. 15.6 miles.

     Paintbrush Canyon is known for its beautiful canyon walls, its meadows, its spotted patches of timber, its beautiful flowers and the terrific surrounding scenery of cliffs and snow slopes in every direction. The combination of traversing Cascade Canyon and Paintbrush Canyon in either direction is considered by many to be one of the most scenic trips in the Tetons.
     From String Lake to Holly Lake and back can be made in one day by a very, very strong hiker.
     The Paintbrush Canyon Trail is less heavily used than the Cascade Canyon Trail but the loop trail using both canyons is becoming increasingly popular. Restrictions to camping are

being made to preserve the natural flora of the area and recently Lake Solitude and Holly Lake have been placed off limits to campers so those desiring to camp along this area must definitely confer with the rangers before carrying out these plans. The loop through these two canyons is very lengthy and beautiful and certainly one should plan on about four days at least with three overnight stops to enjoy the flora and fauna and beautiful scenic vistas which one encounters while going through Cascade Canyon and Paintbrush Canyon in either direction.

The easiest way to get into Paintbrush Canyon is from the picnic area at the end of the road going northwest from Jenny Lake Lodge along the west side of String Lake. From the picnic area a trail takes off that follows along the east shore of String Lake for about a mile where one will come to a bridge that crosses String Lake near the outlet of Leigh Lake. From there one continues straight west until you come to a junction of the trails, one of which goes south along the west side of String Lake to Jenny Lake but the other which we want to take turns right at this junction and goes northwest up through some beautiful timbered country and swings around to the west entering Paintbrush Canyon. At that point where you first hit Paintbrush Canyon Creek, you'll be at an elevation of about 7,600 feet which is nearly a thousand feet above Leigh Lake from where you started. From here the trail climbs up through meadows and scattered timber and rocks, crossing the stream on a bridge, and then continues on the north side of the stream as you continue climbing up the canyon. Along here you will see Mt. Woodring to the northwest with its permanent snow field on the east side and Rock Chuck Peak towards the southeast and Mount St. John to the south of you. After crossing several minor streams coming from the nearby mountains, one climbs up a series of small switchbacks and goes about three quarters of a mile through a patch of timber, where one comes to another trail junction. Both of the trails leading from this junction will join again in about a mile on up the valley. The lower trail goes through the scattered timber and takes a lower route to the right over to Holly Lake which is at an elevation of about 9,400 feet. The left hand trail goes up above the timber below the glaciers and peaks along the south side of the valley and again joins the other trail coming up from Holly Lake. The combined trails then continue almost due west climbing up out of the valley where it becomes very steep as you approach Paintbrush Divide. Here again directly north of the Paintbrush Divide there may be some very steep and dangerous snow fields, especially in the early part of the summer. Anyone except a very experienced mountaineer planning to go over Paintbrush Divide should have previously consulted rangers as to the trail conditions and safety through this area.

Grand Teton from No. Cascade Canyon, Bridger-Teton National Forest photo by Scott Phillips.

LEIGH CANYON — MORAN CANYON ROUTE

USGS Maps: Jenny Lake, Mount Moran.
Distances: Lakes 7785 5 miles, E.R. 6.8 miles.
            Mink Lake 8 miles, E.R. 12.1 miles.
            Divide 9.3 miles, E.R. 15.6 miles.
            Cirque Creek 12.3 miles, E.R. 18.6 miles.
            Moran Bay 16.8 miles, E.R. 23.1 miles.
            Bearpaw Lake 20 miles, E.R. 26.5 miles.
            Picnic Area Beginning 24 miles, E.R. 30.5 miles.

For the experienced backpacker who wants to get away from it all, I would recommend the back country around Mt. Moran. At this writing, while many of the trails near the Grand Teton and Jenny Lake are crowded with people, I have in the recent past spent two weeks in the back country around Mt. Moran without seeing one tourist. Leigh Canyon is one of the places to get away from it all. However, one will have to pay the price with some rough traveling, but the rewards in wilderness hiking and camping are well worth the effort. The trip up Leigh Canyon starts near the Jenny Lake Lodge where one will cross the bridge near the outlet of String Lake and go on the trail to the south where soon one will hit the String Lake Trail and go along the west side of String Lake towards the north. Or, one can start at the picnic area at the end of the road leading northwest from the Jenny Lake Lodge on the east side of String Lake. From the picnic area, one will go north along the east shore of String Lake to the bridge and cross near the outlet of Leigh Lake. From the bridge one would go straight west and climb to join the String Lake Trail. From this junction, one goes north and west traversing around the mountain on the Paintbrush Canyon Trail. This trail traverses the northern slopes of the mountains on the south side of Leigh Lake. You follow the Paintbrush Canyon Trail from the junction with the String Lake Trail for about a mile and a half to a point where you'll be approximately straight south of the west end of Leigh Lake which you can see below you through the timber towards the north. At that point, start traveling north and a little bit west towards the western tip of Leigh Lake. In about half a mile you will cross the stream coming out of Paintbrush Canyon and continue on towards the north where you will approach the creek coming out of Leigh Canyon near where it runs into Leigh Lake.

Keep on the north side of the stream where there is a primitive path going up the canyon. However, you'll probably be in big boulders and downed timber interspersed with trees, and for an hour or two you are going to be in a labyrinth of rocks and bushwacking terrain. You will soon understand why very few people take the hike up Leigh Canyon. However, if you persist when you think all is hopeless and finished, you will come upon clearings where you can walk over fairly easy boulders and along a very beautiful stream and hit a couple of small lakes at approximately 7,800 feet in elevation. You will be rewarded in the meantime by seeing the perpendicular south walls of Mt. Moran which are extremely spectacular. Also, to the north of these little lakes are beautiful little glacial cirques and Thor Peak above. It was on Thor Peak that I at one time made a first ascent and named it Thor Peak, for some reason or other, but that was in the distant past.

For mountaineers, this is one of the more interesting ways of climbing Mt. Moran because one can take a fairly easy route around the west side of Thor Peak and more or less follow the Black Dike that goes all the way to the top of Mt. Moran. This is a very interesting and wonderful trip.

Continuing on up the canyon, one will be in a very, very wild trail-less canyon where one should see game in a canyon that's filled with beautiful flowers and extraordinary scenery.

I would think that if one got up to the two small lakes through the labyrinth of brush and rocks at the bottom of Leigh Canyon, that would be enough for the first day. On the second day, one can go on up the canyon possibly as far as Mink Lake, which sits in a narrow basin at approximately 8,900 feet. You have come approximately six or seven miles up this canyon without gaining much elevation. However, that shouldn't encourage the hiker too much because plenty of strength will be exerted going over fallen logs, through boulder fields and across various obstacles that you will encounter along this route.

From Mink Lake one can go towards the northwest to a saddle at approximately 10,000 feet that will lead over into the drainage of the south fork of Moran Creek where one will be in perhaps the most isolated part of the Grand Teton Park. Any people that you might encounter in this area will be experienced hikers and mountaineers who have earned their right to be in this beautiful solitude. All around you will be beautiful small peaks to climb. One can travel on down the south fork of Moran Creek until he comes to the junction of the stream flowing out of Cirque Lake. A hike up to Cirque Lake about a mile and a half to two miles south and camping in that vicinity in the scattered timber around the lake would be a well-rewarded experience. This lake sits in a beautiful isolated cirque below the peaks, cliffs, and glaciers to the south of it.

One can continue on down Moran Canyon where one will have very, very spectacular views to the south of Renolds, Traverse, and Bivouac Peaks. Also, going down this canyon looking to the south you will see the west and south sides of Mt. Moran, and Triple Glaciers below it. This view of Mt. Moran is one that very few tourists in the Grand Tetons ever get.

Going down Moran Creek, one can find various game trails and going will not be as difficult as coming up Leigh Creek. Perhaps one might find an old trail along the north side of Moran Canyon along the edge of the meadows and below the trees coming down most of the canyon. Moran Creek, at the bottom of the canyon, runs into Moran Bay in Jackson Lake and if you don't have a boat to pick you up, God help you. Gad, what country this is! Can you imagine the isolation of this country back here where nobody ever goes. Nobody ever goes in there.

When one traverses Leigh Canyon to its upper end and crosses up into Moran Canyon and descends to Moran Bay, one should have enough time to enjoy the Pristine Wilderness and scenic beauties of this area without being on any definite schedule. Therefore, it would be difficult to arrange for a boat to meet you in Moran Bay, so there is another way to come out. Following game trails and using your best experience at route finding, you can follow above the shore line of Moran Bay and go to the south until you get into Bear Paw Bay, which is a very deep inlet in Jackson Lake, where at its southern extremity a stream comes in which you can follow up to Bear Paw Lake. On the south side of Bear Paw Lake, you'll find a trail leading over to the north end of Leigh Lake past a patrol cabin. This is the beginning of the Valley Trail which you can follow back along the east side of Leigh Lake to the lower end of Leigh Lake to the picnic area from where you started. This is a very, very pleasant one week trip and one would be ill advised to push it and try to make it in any less than six days.

Mules Ears, Bridger-Teton National Forest photo by Perkins

GRASSY L.

Reclamation Road

LAKE OF THE WOODS

FLAGG RANCH

SNAKE R.

SO. BOONE

BERRY CR.

89 287

N

ELK RIDGE

JACKASS PASS

BERRY CR.

CONANT PASS

OWL CR.

OWL P.

0 1 2

SCALE

NO. BITCH

MOOSE BASIN DIVIDE

WEBB CANYON

NORD P.

SO. BITCH

MOOSE BASIN

HIDDEN CORRAL BASIN

CAMP L.

JACKSON LAKE

RAMMEL MTN.

DEAD HORSE PASS

SO. BADGER

GREEN MTN.

MORAN CANYON

CIRQUE L.

MT. MORAN

BASIN L.

THOR

LEIGH L.

LEIGH CANYON

Teton Park, North

BERRY CREEK TRAIL

USGS Maps: Huckleberry Mountain, Colter Bay
Distances: Reclamation Road to Berry Creek Tr. Jct. 4.5 miles,
 E.R. 5 miles.
 Berry Creek Patrol Cabin 7.2 miles, E.R. 7.7 miles.
 Survey Peak Divide 11.5 miles, E.R. 14.8 miles.
 Forellen Peak Divide 12.5 miles, E.R. 16.8 miles.
 Jackass Pass 12.5 miles, E.R. 15.8 miles.
 Conant Pass 13 miles, E.R. 17 miles.
Note: These distances in miles and Energy Rated miles is
 about the same whether starting from the Reclama-
 tion Road or the Berry Creek Patrol Cabin on
 Jackson Lake.

As in the other canyons and creeks that run into Jackson Lake, boats can be arranged for at the various concessions. and boat landings that surround Jackson Lake for transportation to various points around Jackson Lake. Arrangements can be made for pickups at specific times at the end of ones journey.

However, in order to reach Berry Creek, if you don't use a boat, you can hike in from Reclamation Road which begins at Flagg Ranch, about two miles south of the south entrance to Yellowstone Park. Coming up from Teton National Park, you reach the Flagg Ranch just after you cross the Snake River and it is located to the left just off the main highway. This road is well marked.

The road that one would take to reach the entrance to Berry Creek is known as the Reclamation Road and it is a road that is passable by automobiles, running from the Flagg Ranch to Ashton, Idaho. This road runs west from the Flagg Ranch for about a mile where it crosses Pole Cat Creek. Just across the bridge you turn south and proceed for about two more miles and then the road swings west again for another mile or so towards the Grassy Lake Reservoir before you reach the spot where the trail takes off to the south going down to Berry Creek. There is a Forest Service Ranger Station just west of Flagg Ranch where you can get road and trail information.

Backpacking the Northern Tetons, Jackson Hole News photo
by G. Bellerose

This trail to Berry Creek begins as an old logging road and proceeds south for a little over a mile where it comes out along the marshy meadows bordering the Snake River above where it enters Jackson Lake. Following along the edge of the meadows and below the trees, you proceed south for another mile and a half where you'll walk along the northwest side of Jackson Lake for about a mile. Here the trail swings off towards the west where in about a mile you will join the trail that goes up Berry Creek. The beginning or the lower end of this trail does not follow Berry Creek itself but heads up to the west over a divide along the north end of Elk Ridge where you'll cross over into the Berry Creek Drainage and be on the Berry Creek Trail. Back where these trails divide, if you took the left branch, you would continue south onto another small stream which runs down and empties into Jackson Lake. There is some fair fishing in the small lakes and stream for brook and cutthroat trout. Proceeding on to the south, you will cross this small stream and then in about a mile further, you will reach a patrol cabin where Berry Creek enters Jackson Lake. Here one should find good fishing in the streams and near the outlets of the streams in Jackson Lake. Approximately a quarter or half a mile south of the patrol cabin and just a few hundred yards south of where Berry Creek enters the lake, one will also find Moose Creek where it enters the lake. It comes down Webb Canyon and enters Jackson Lake near where Berry Creek enters. Moose Creek should also be good fishing at various times of the year.

From the patrol cabin, the trail goes west along the north side of Berry Creek and there should be good fishing all along in the holes and rapids and meadows for the entire length of the creek. Approximately three miles above the patrol cabin one will come to some marshy areas in the meadows along the creek where one will find beaver dams which are also excellent places to fish. Here the stream will meander around and through the willows and beaver dams for approximately one mile to where one will find the junction of Owl Creek and Berry Creek. This vicinity reports excellent fishing. Behind the beaver dams one will find nice pan sized brook trout and also there will be cutthroat trout in the streams. There is good fishing for another mile or two up Owl Creek to the left.

The trail that goes up Berry Creek crosses Berry Creek at the head of the marsh-like region and goes up the hill a ways on the west side of the stream and swings off to the right, going up the canyon where the trail will be above the stream for about a mile. Here the trail will cross the stream and head back towards the east for a short distance before joining the other trail coming from Jackson Lake. Joining this trail you will turn sharply to the left and proceed towards the north and west, staying above the north side of Berry Creek where in about a mile one will again hit a marshy meandering stream where one will again find beaver ponds and good fishing. The trail follows along bordering the marshy area above the stream for a little over three miles where the trail divides, the right fork going steeply up the canyon to the right of Survey Peak where in about a mile or so it crosses the divide leading over into South Boone Creek.

Proceeding on up Berry Creek about another half a mile from the junction you'll pass a patrol cabin near the stream. Proceeding to the west from this patrol cabin and staying on the south side of Berry Creek, the trail heads towards the south climbing gradually up along the east side of Berry Creek for about a mile before climbing more steeply for another mile to where it reaches a pass that goes over into Owl Creek. This is an old non-maintained trail and from here, you may follow it over to Forellen Peak and on to the east, back to Berry Creek. A faint, rough trail descends to Owl Creek from the pass, but is difficult to follow.

From near the patrol cabin on the north side of Berry Creek a trail takes off to the west and climbs up to what is known as Jackass Pass in about a mile and a half. Here you will connect with trails leading to different areas on the west side of the divide. Some of these are South Boone Creek, Hominy Creek, Conant Creek, Grizzly Creek and North Bitch Creek Trails and trails going down many other drainages which go into the north fork of the Snake River and do not drain into Jackson Hole or the south fork of the Snake River.

Moose Basin, Jackson Hole News photo by G. Bellerose

OWL CREEK TRAIL

USGS Maps: Colter Bay, Huckleberry Mountain, Grassy Lake
        Reservoir, Ranger Peak.
Distances: Berry Creek Ranger Sta. to Owl Creek 3.2 miles,
        E.R. 3.8 miles.
        Moose Basin Divide 10.2 miles, E.R. 16 miles.

Hiking in the north end of Grand Teton National Park around Berry, Owl and Moose Creeks is extremely rewarding to people who want to be in a gentle country with lots of flora and fauna. One should see a number of deer, elk and moose in this vicinity. The fishing is good in many places. The trees, meadows and the flowers are outstanding and there generally are not very many people in this region.

At the junction of Owl Creek and Berry Creek which is at an elevation of about 7,200 feet, one could proceed to the west and follow the Owl Creek Trail. The first mile of this trail follows the meandering stream, past beaver ponds where good fishing can be anticipated. Proceeding west, you follow the creek quite closely for several miles, crossing it occasionally. As the creek turns towards the south, the trail follows it to the upper reaches of the creek where it finally heads eastward climbing up away from the stream and eventually reaches Moose Basin Divide at an elevation of nearly 10,000 feet. From here the trail continues through the divide going southward for a short distance before swinging to the east and following the Webb Canyon Trail. This traverses the upper reaches of Moose Basin and continues on down past the patrol cabin, down Webb Canyon through which flows Moose Creek which empties into Jackson Lake.

Moose Basin, Jackson Hole News photo by G. Bellerose

WEBB CANYON TRAIL

USGS Maps: Colter Bay, Ranger Peak.
Distances: Moose Basin Patrol Cabin 8 miles, E.R. 11.6 miles.
          Moose Basin Divide 10 miles, E.R. 15.9 miles.
          Moose Mountain Pass 9.5 miles, E.R. 15.4 miles.

From near the patrol cabin at the mouth of Berry Creek the trail takes off to the west and then turns south along the flat marshy area near Jackson Lake and in about three quarters of a mile reaches Moose Creek, After the trail reaches Moose Creek, it continues to follow it generally along the north side going up Webb Canyon. This trail follows along the stream crossing it occasionally for seven or eight miles where near the upper end, it passes near some beautiful falls and proceeds on about another three quarters of a mile to a patrol cabin. This cabin is in the lower reaches of Moose Basin. Here the trail goes northwesterly up out of the canyon and climbs up to Moose Basin Divide at approximately 10,000 feet. Here, one can cross over and follow the Owl Creek Trail back down to Jackson Lake near the patrol cabin from where one started.

From the area near the patrol cabin at the lower part of Moose Basin, one can make his way generally towards the west up the drainage and cross over just to the south of Moose Mountain through a low saddle. Here one can cross over onto the west side of the mountains and a trail starting here goes down to Nord Pass where it joins the trail coming up North Bitch Creek. This trail, if you follow it to the south, will take you down to Camp Lake and from there on to the west down into the South Bitch Creek Drainage. Also, one could probably make his way from the Moose Basin Divide south along the east side of the wall and cross over either on the north or south side of Moose Mountain and proceed over to the North Bitch Creek Trail.

Bridger - Teton National Forest

The Bridger-Teton National Forest encompasses three sides of famed Jackson Hole which was named for Davey Jackson, a partner in the Rocky Mountain Fur Company. Portions of this National Forest were included in the original Yellowstone Park Timber Land Reserve, established March 30, 1891, the first public forest reservation in the United States.

The Bridger Division of the National Forest is named for Jim Bridger, famous mountain man, explorer, and partner in the Rocky Mountain Fur Company which flourished during the early part of the 19th century.

The Bridger and Teton National Forests merged as one on July 1, 1973. Headquarters for this National Forest is in Jackson, Wyoming.

Only a small portion of the Bridger-Teton National Forest is included in this guide. This is located north of the Teton Pass Highway 22, between it and the Teton National Park boundary along the crest of Rendezvous Mountain. Trails included are: the beginning of our High Adventure Trail which is the Phillips Pass Trail, Phillips Canyon Trail, and the beginning of the Rendezvous Mountain Trail which starts on the aerial Tramway in Teton Village.

No reservations or registering is necessary for hiking this section of the Teton Range.

I wish to speak a word for Nature,
for absolute freedom and wilderness.

—Henry David Thoreau

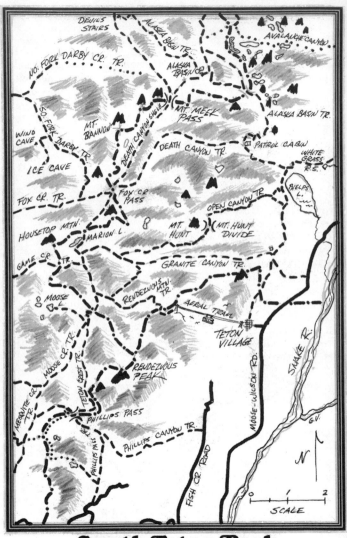

South Teton Park

PHILLIPS PASS TRAIL

USGS Maps: Teton Village, Rendezvous Peak
Distances: Phillips Pass 5 miles, E.R. 10.3 miles.

This is a pretty canyon, not heavily used, that leads up to Phillips Pass where it joins the Teton Crest Trail. A loop trail would take you out on the Phillips Pass Trail to the highway below Teton Pass. (See Phillips Pass Trail.)

To get to the trailhead, you drive to Wilson, west of Jackson, and turn north off the highway onto a paved road directly across from the Fish Creek Inn. Go one block and turn right. Go one block and turn left. You will now be heading north on Fish Creek Road which is a paved country road. Go a little over three miles to where on the left side will be an old post in the ground and a gate. There is a small turn-out parking place on the right side of the road. This is where the trail starts. There is no sign here as you have to cross private property. Permission to cross has been granted all hikers so you won't have any problem and you don't have to ask.

The trail is pretty gentle for the first mile and a half as it follows the stream. Then it climbs above the stream and rises fairly fast the rest of the way. It goes up Middle Fork and there the Phillips Pass Trail joins it. Then it proceeds on to the pass.

. . . I have been a tree amid the wood
And many a new thing understood
That was rank folly to my head before.

—Ezra Pound

PHILLIPS CANYON TRAIL

USGS Map: Rendezvous Peak.
Distances: Ski Lake 2 miles, E.R. 3.7 miles.
           Phillips Pass 4 miles, E.R. 6.3 miles.
           Moose Creek Divide 8.5 miles, E.R. 13.5 miles.
           Phillips Pass - Ski Lake Loop 3.5 miles, E.R. 5.1
           miles.

This trail can be used as an interesting one day loop trail or as one of the access trails to the Teton Crest and Skyline Trail.

The trail begins on an old logging road which takes off from the Teton Pass Highway a short ways west of where it crosses the North Fork of Trail Creek on the east side of the pass. There is a sign there indicating "Phillips Canyon".

The trail begins about three fourths of a mile up this road, on the left. There is a large open sagebrush covered hillside on the left. The trail goes up through that and parallels the road, about 200 feet up. The start is a little difficult to find but by careful searching it can be located. If you can't find it, just go up the open hillside and you'll come across it.

The trail climbs up a short distance onto a small bench, follows it aways, and then climbs some more. In less than a mile you'll come out of the trees into an open area and cross a stream going down Phillips Canyon. Just across this stream a trail takes off to the left and goes up to Ski Lake, a little over a mile away. It is a pretty lake setting in a cirque with trees on one side and open on the other. This is a nice place to camp or picnic.

Going ahead on the main trial, you traverse about a half mile and cross another creek. This one comes out of Ski Lake. Another mile or so and you'll cross the Middle Fork of Phillips Creek where the Phillips Canyon Trail joins from the right. Another mile of gradual climbing will bring you to Phillips Pass where you'll join the Teton Crest Trail. Going on, the Teton Crest Trail goes around the base of Rendezvous Peak and in about four miles joins the trail coming up Moose Creek. This four mile section isn't a really good trail but you should be able to follow it.

From Phillips Pass you can drop down to Mesquite Creek and go out on Moose Creek. The easiest loop trail is taking another route back to Ski Lake.

To take the loop trail back to Ski Lake, from Phillips Pass you head off to the west, staying on the south side of the ridge in the open. You traverse clear around a big bowl, staying near the crest all the way until you're looking down a very prominent canyon to the east. Ski Lake is down this canyon. You can see a trail wandering down this canyon and it goes to Ski Lake. From the lake you follow the trail down to join Phillips Pass Trail about a half mile from your car. This loop trail could easily be done in one day.

From about half way along the crest going west and south from Phillips Pass, another trail follows a ridge to the west and joins the end of the Coal Creek Trail at elevation 9197 feet. This is part of another loop trail using Phillips Pass Trail and Coal Creek Trail.

Wilderness Camping, Bridger-Teton National Forest photo by Scott Phillips

Targhee National Forest Trails

In the summer of 1877, white men and a band of Nezperce Indians fought a skirmish at Henry's Lake. According to the account, famed Chief Joseph was attempting to stave off a group of soldiers and thereby provide time for his people to escape through Yellowstone into Canada.

During the fracas two or three Indians were killed, and a short way off among the trees several squaws began to wail, "Targhee, Targhee". One report has it that an Indian named Targhee was among those slain—another that he was either a chief, warrior, or guide whom the women were calling for help. Still another account related that Targhee (originally "Ty-gee") was a Bannock chief killed by Crow Indians in the winter of 1871-72.

Whatever the facts, there is fairly uniform agreement that Targhee was an Indian of stature and courage, respected by his people. It was in honor of this man that a number of landmarks were named—a pass, a peak, a creek, and in 1908, one of America's National Forests.

The Targhee National Forest extends in a great semi-circle around the headwaters of the Snake River in eastern Idaho and western Wyoming. Its 1.7 million acres take in a vast sweep of mountains and valleys northward and westward from the Grand Canyon of the Snake and the crest of the Teton Peaks to the little Lost River. North and south, it extends from the Continental Divide to the edge of the Upper Snake River Valley.

GENERAL BACKPACKING AND HIKING INFORMATION

Hiking on the west side of the Tetons can be very rewarding because the country has beautiful timber and heavily flowered meadows. That side of the mountain receives more rain and consequently the vegetation is more lush than that on the eastern slopes of the Tetons. Certainly the most interesting fact to wilderness hikers is that the western slopes are much less heavily used than the more popular trails going down the eastern canyons. More use should certainly be made of traversing from the Idaho side across the top into the Wyoming side. One can also find all along the divide separating Idaho from Wyoming a series of cliffs and small mountain peaks as well as boulder fields where one can practice bouldering and climbing.

A nice thing about the west side and especially up high in the North and South Bitch and South Badger and Granite Basin area is that this is the divide of the watershed and it's kind of a mellow rolling area where one can see right into the big peaks of Mt. Moran and Owen and the Grand and Middle Teton.

The overall country on the west side is more mild than the major peaks of the Tetons. In hiking you don't gain as much elevation because you start higher up and except for getting out of the canyons, the walking isn't bad.

There is very little granite on the west side. There is granite in Granite Basin, Bitch Creek Narrows and around Mt. Nord. Otherwise, the western slope is all limestone and one can see the uplift of the beds. Geologically, it is very interesting. It seems to have wide canyons that appear U-shaped and may have been formed by glaciers.

The western slopes are tremendous for its variety of flowers and lush vegetation. Sometimes you can get into a field of corn lillies that are ten feet high. The avalanche paths keep some of the slopes clear of trees but this provides wide open areas where wild flowers abound.

A few restrictions on trail use do apply. All refuse should be packed out. Short-cutting trails, such as across switch backs, is not allowed. No motorized vehicles are allowed on the South Fork of Teton Canyon Trail, and no open fires are allowed in Alaska Basin in the canyon's upper end. At present, however, campfires are allowed in all other areas on the District. Camping and fire permits are not required.

Trails on the district begin opening up about the first of July, although higher trails on the West Slope of the Tetons may open up much later. High water makes many trails on the West Slope hazardous well into July, and unforeseen events such as snowslides sometimes make trails impassable until late season.

TYPES OF HIKING EXPERIENCE
Opportunities on Targhee National Forest are nearly unlimited. They range from short, easy hikes for the novice or the physically limited, to rugged backpacking trips, or extended remote area trips with commercial guide service.

TRAIL CONDITIONS
Check with the local District Ranger office. Due to lack of funds the trails are not always well maintained.

FEES
No fees are charged for use of the trails.

CAMPGROUNDS
No campground facilities on the back country trails.

MOTORIZED VEHICLES
A few trails prohibit use of motorized vehicles. Check with the local District Ranger office before leaving on your trip.

STAY LIMIT
There is no limit of stay in the back country.

PARTY SIZE LIMIT
The only limit of size of party presently in effect is a limit of 25 horses for commercial outfitters.

FIRE PERMITS
Fire permits are not presently required for camp cooking fires on the Targhee. All fire precautionary measures should be adhered to.

WEATHER
Best weather months are July, August and the first part of September, with August the driest. Any time after September 10 sudden temperature drops and early snow storms at the higher elevations can occur.

Note: The trail distances are given in miles and Energy Rated (E.R.) miles. For each 500 feet of elevation gained, one mile is added to the distance. The result (E.R.) combines the actual miles with the climbing, to indicate the energy needed for each trail.

COAL CREEK TRAIL

USGS Map: Rendezvous Peak
Distances: Mesquite Canyon Divide 2.6 miles, E.R. 4.6 miles.
          Moose Meadows 4.6 miles, E.R. 6.6 miles.
          Phillips Pass 4.6 miles, E.R. 7 miles.

Coal Creek serves as a popular entry point onto the high trails known collectively as the Teton Crest Trail and which I have called my "High Adventure Trail". My description of that trail begins on the Phillips Pass Trail on the east side of Teton Pass.

The Coal Creek Trail is well maintained and usually uncrowded. It has been getting quite a lot of use primarily as a day trip where hikers make the loop up Coal Creek and come back on the Phillips Pass Trial. This is done by going up Coal Creek to the pass between Mesquite and Coal Creek, then going east up the ridge and then north over to Phillips Pass and return on the Phillips Pass Trail.

The Coak Creek Trail begins at the Coak Creek Campground which is signed about two miles west of Teton Pass on Highway 22 going from Victor, Idaho to Jackson Hole, Wyoming. This is not an official campground as such but there are plenty of places to park your car or camp overnight if you wish. The trailhead has a sign on it simply stating "Coal Creek Trail".

Starting at the campground, the trail climbs gradually with some steep sections here and there before you reach the pass at the head of the creek in about 2½ miles. It is a really nice trail because it parallels the creek for a lot of the way. The stream is fast moving with a lot of little waterfalls.

Coal Creek Meadows is a very pretty place to camp. It is a large flat area filled with flowers and grass with a huge spring coming out in it. For additional scenery, you're looking right up at Taylor Mountain.

Just before reaching the pass, a sign at a trail junction points left where the Taylor Mountain Trail takes off. This trail is pretty rugged as it climbs steeply to the top of Taylor Mountain about a thousand feet higher in about a mile.

At the pass between Coal and Mesquite Creek an old trail no longer maintained takes off to the east up the ridge and over to Phillips Pass about two miles away. This trail has a lot of downed timber on it but a lot of people use it.

Going on over onto Mesquite Creek, there are some steep sections as you proceed about two miles to Moose Meadows. Just before the trail gets into Moose Meadows and joins the trail up Moose Creek, you go around large beaver ponds. There is a difficult crossing where the water comes out of these big beaver ponds.

See the Moose Creek Trail description for continued information.

Hidden Corral Basin, Teton Trails Photography

TAYLOR MOUNTAIN TRAIL

USGS Maps: Driggs, Rendezvous Peak.
Distances: Taylor Basin 5 miles, E.R. 9.4 miles.
   Taylor Mountain 6.5 miles, E.R. 13.3 miles.

   This is a real nice day hike up an easy trail to Taylor Basin, which is a very beautiful grassy cirque full of flowers. There are nine camping or lunch spots along the streams and some springs if you can find them.
   The Taylor Mountain Trail begins at Nordwall Campground, up Moose Creek. The road up Moose Creek leaves the highway about three miles southeast of Victor, Idaho and is signed. Drive up the Moose Creek road and take the right fork not too long after it makes a creek crossing and it takes you to Nordwall Campground. Signs here indicate the Taylor Mountain Trail goes up an old road to the right leading up to a mill. Up the old road a ways, there's a sign showing where the trail leaves the road and goes on up to Taylor Mountain.
   It's an easy trail, about three miles or so and takes you up to a big cirque known as Taylor Basin. The trail contours along at the beginning for quite a ways, then drops into the head of Bear Canyon, crosses over through the head of another canyon and then drops into Taylor Basin. Through the basin it's fairly level but soon the trail starts to climb and gets pretty steep as you near the top of Taylor Mountain.
   You can make a loop trail by going on over Taylor Mountain and down to the Coal Creek Trail on the other side. Either approach to the mountain is difficult. Climbing up out of Taylor Basin or up out of Coal Creek is a steep hike.

MOOSE CREEK TRAIL

USGS Maps: Driggs, Rendezvous Peak.
Distances: Moose Meadows 4 miles, E.R. 5.7 miles.
         Teton Crest Trail 7 miles, E.R. 11.1 miles.

The Moose Creek Trail offers access to fishing, the largest waterfall on the west slope of the Tetons, and spectacular lakes high in the head of the canyon. It is an easy trail and well maintained. It is heavily used by horse riders, day hikers, and backpackers using it as an access to the Teton Crest Trail. Early in the season the crossing above Moose Meadows is a little difficult and you can count on doing some wading in fast water. This crossing would not be recommended for the less adventurous.

Go up the Moose Creek road which is signed where it turns off from the highway about three miles southeast of Victor, Idaho. Turn right at the fork about a mile and a half in and proceed to the Nordwall Campground. Follow the road past the campground over to Bear Canyon. From there on the road is very poor and it is suggested that you park your car in the Bear Canyon area or back at Nordwall Campground.

The trail follows the old road and continues on up Moose Creek. It is a good trail, well maintained, with only gradual climbing all the way to Moose Meadows at the head of the canyon. It is a pretty canyon, has good water and fishing all the way. There are numerous good camping places all along the canyon.

The trail to the meadows follows the stream, through open areas and past an occasional beaver pond and you'll arrive at the meadows after hiking about five miles.

At Moose Meadows there actually isn't much of a meadow. There are some nice campsites on the northeast side of the ponds. There's also one on the other side of the creek, on the southwest side. Primarily the trail stays on the high ground along the northwest side of the meadow, passing above or around most of the wet, boggy area. There is good fishing in the ponds along here.

The trail going on up Moose Creek from the meadows climbs gradually until you reach the switchbacks in the upper end of the canyon. There are some falls about two miles above the meadows which are really spectacular. They are the biggest on this side of the Teton Range. These are difficult to see from the trail. Actually they drop away from right beside the trail. The trail goes up over some cliffs right above the falls. They are in a notch, dropping down through these cliffs. There are two large falls, one above the other. If you're not looking for them you could walk right past without ever seeing them.

Just before the trail joins the Teton Crest Trail near the Park boundary, a trail takes off to the left going over to Moose Lakes. There is no sign on it and it is not maintained. It is an obvious trail and a well beaten path going off to the left. It's about two miles up to several lakes sitting on different shelves. The largest, Moose Lake, has quite a few small fish in it and it's good fishing. There is a big bench up there with several lakes on the same level as the main one. You have to go up through some cliffs to get onto the bench but it's a real easy trail. The water from Moose Lake goes roaring down into a big hole in the ground and it's pretty spectacular.

Going on up Moose Creek Trail you come to a sign at the Park boundary in a saddle passing through the crest of the Tetons. Here the Moose Creek Trail ends as you join the Teton Crest Trail. The sign gives mileages to various places. Going ahead you'd soon reach the Middle Fork Cut Off trail leading to the Rendezvous Mountain Trail which goes down Granite Canyon. Further on you'd reach Marion Lake and go on to Fox Creek Pass. The trail just across the divide isn't in very good shape. It pretty much just goes up and down the slopes without any switchbacks. Early in the season it's muddy and slick.

GAME CREEK TRAIL

USGS Maps: Driggs, Rendezvous Peak
Distances: Teton Divide 6.9 miles, E.R. 13.9 miles.
           Teton Crest Trail 8 miles, E.R. 14.9 miles.
           Housetop Mountain 8 miles, E.R. 16 miles.

One attraction for this trail is its access to Housetop Mountain where there is a very nice view of the lakes on the east of the divide. Also there are some fossils of ancient sea life to be found in the canyon. The main attraction is that the area is isolated and very few people use it. There is no fishing here so the hikers have it to themselves. The trail gets only occasional maintenance and is in only fair condition but most of it is easy hiking. It is not one of the easiest to follow because of lack of use. There are rock cairns and tree blazes that will guide the experienced hiker.

The road leading into Game Creek leaves from the old highway about two and a half miles southeast of Victor, Idaho. On the old road there is a sign indicating Game Creek but there is no sign on the road going up this creek. The road passes between houses on each side with side roads leading to them so it's a little difficult to find the right road, but keep going up the canyon about a mile. At the trail head there has been built a small dam on the stream for a gravity flow sprinkler system. There is a sign on the trail here and there is adequate parking for cars. The trail starts on the north side of the creek and you cross on a log bridge to get on it.

The trail begins climbing gradually and follows the stream all the way to the crest of the Tetons where it climbs steeply to the ridge. The creek is a very nice clear fast flowing stream but not a very large one.

In the upper end of the canyon there are some large cirques and several fairly high peaks towering above them. Crossing over the divide, the trail drops down to join the Teton Crest Trail about a mile below, down the trail from Marion Lake.

To get to Housetop Mountain which is the one towering above you north of the upper cirque, follow the ridge to the north along the divide right up to the top. From there you'll see Marion Lake about a mile east of you, and the entire Teton Range on up the divide.

The South Fork of Game Creek is used mainly by sheep herders and the trail leading into it is not maintained.

The North Fork also has a trail leading some distance up it but it is not maintained and would be difficult to follow.

FOX CREEK TRAIL

USGS Maps: Driggs, Mount Bannon
Distances: South Darby Trail Junction 7 miles, E.R. 11 miles.
          Fox Creek Pass 8 miles, E.R. 13.6 miles.

Fox Creek is one of the most beautiful canyons in the area. It is really narrow in contrast to the others on this side of the Tetons. Most of the other canyons seem to have been made by glacial action whereas Fox Creek seems to have been cut by itself. Along this stream are some small beaver ponds containing deep crystal clear water. Some fish and a lot of wildlife may be found here, particularly moose, as well as some coyote, deer and elk. The open meadows along the canyon are good places for camping. Near the upper end there are some large caves.

This trail is not recommended during the early summer because of hazardous stream crossings, but later in the summer is one of the better routes. It is used only moderately.

The road leading up Fox Creek leaves the main highway three miles north of Victor and five miles south of Driggs, Idaho. It's signed as the Fox Creek Road. The road enters the canyon after about 2½ miles.

There is a small bit of private land enclosed by the National Forest in this canyon and it is being actively used as a rock quarry. The road going up the canyon is a good road and is maintained by the people running the quarry. Hikers using this road should be on the lookout for large trucks carrying heavy loads of limestone. At the border of the private property, they

123

have built a parking lot for hikers using the trail. This parking lot is off to the right as you reach a large gate on the road. A little trail leads back up onto the road from the parking lot.

The trail follows the road until you get up to the quarry where you'll cross the creek on a log bridge near a settling pond. There is a sign here indicating the trailhead. You'll follow up this new trail a ways and you'll cross the stream again on a log bridge. This new trail continues for quite a distance, then drops down into a fairly flat area along the bottom of the canyon.

Spearhead Peak, Teton Trails Photography.

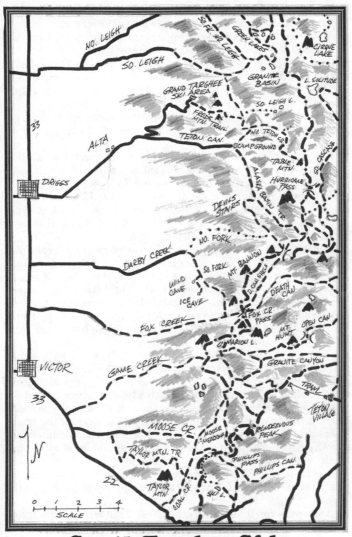

South Targhee Side

125

This large meadow is an extremely beautiful place, with a patch of quakies, and beaver activity along the stream.

Above here there are several stream crossings that can be hazardous so you should take care at these places.

Continuing on up the stream, you'll climb gradually for a couple of miles and then the trail gets steeper as you climb out the last three miles. There is a small falls on the stream off to the right of the trail along one of the steeper sections.

In the upper reaches of the canyon it opens up into large meadows with meandering streams where there are a lot of nice places to camp.

There is a cliff band that follows along the north side all the way up the canyon containing natural caves. About a half mile above the falls the trail forks. The left fork goes up into the cliffs. As you reach the cliffs, the biggest cave is located off to the left a few hundred yards. This is a horizontal, walk-in type cave that is reported to go in a thousand feet. Several others along here invite careful exploring.

The left fork trail going near the caves goes on over into Darby Canyon. It is not a constructed trail but is there from use of people crossing over from one canyon to the other. It is not maintained but is easy to follow by foot hikers but is not recommended for horses. This trail is the easy route to the top of Fossil Mountain. When you reach the high point of the trail, just turn right and follow the ridge on up to the top. From this peak you have an exceptional view of the entire Teton Range.

Going on up the main trail to Fox Creek Pass you have most of the real steep part behind you, back near the falls. After that the canyon opens up and the climbing is pretty gradual. Fox Creek Pass is an interesting area with a lot of meadows. A lot of people don't camp there because they don't see any water. There is plenty of water just up to the north a ways off the trail. There are several springs here but the water soon runs back into the rocks. These aren't along the trail but kind of to the northwest a little ways, right at the divide.

Pass Lake is mostly a mud pond but the area around here is nice. Spearhead Peak is the spectacular spine just to the south of you.

At the pass you'll join the Teton Crest Trail which came from

Phillips Pass to the south and continues across onto the Death Canyon Shelf heading for Alaska Basin. Also the Death Canyon Trail joins the Teton Crest Trail at the pass.

On a loop trail using Fox Creek, the easier way would be going up Darby Creek and coming down Fox Creek because the steeper trails are in Fox Creek and you would be going down them. Another nice loop trail would be up Teton Canyon, across Death Canyon Shelf, and down Fox Canyon.

DARBY CREEK TRAIL

USGS Maps: Driggs, Mount Bannon
Distances: Wind Cave 2.7 miles, E.R. 6.2 miles.
          Ice Cave 3.4 miles, E.R. 8 miles.
          Teton Divide 4.5 miles, E.R. 9.7 miles.
          Fox Creek Trail 4.5 miles, E.R. 10.5 miles.

The main attraction of this trail is the wind and ice caves and the loop trail going over and down Fox Creek. Also a route goes up to the divide overlooking upper Teton Creek near Mount Meek. The South Darby Trail is heavily used and is not recommended for those seeking the solitude of a true wilderness experience.

The Darby Creek Road leaves the main highway three miles south of Driggs and five miles north of Victor, Idaho. It's almost three miles to the entrance of the canyon where a good gravel road goes quite a ways on up Darby Creek. You drive clear to the end of the road where there is a parking area, a trailhead sign and a footbridge crossing the stream.

It is nearly three miles of very gradual trail up to the Wind Cave. It is well maintained and an easy hike. The trail comes up the canyon a ways and then switchbacks up until it's going along the top of a cliff. All along here you can see the huge opening to the cave with water coming out. It is a large horizontal cave, going in close to a thousand feet.

As you go into the cave, it narrows down until it finally reaches a size that you have to crawl on your stomach to get through. This is where it gets its name as there is a strong cold wind coming through that hole. The water is only near the entrance but in the spring there is quite a heavy flow and you will need to use caution climbing along the edge to get past it.

The Ice Cave is about a mile south along the same cliff, with many small caves between them. Right along the bottom of the cliff there is a small trail that leads on to the Ice Cave which is at the top of a steep scree slope in the cliff. The Ice Cave has a very small opening with a large rock in front of it so you have to look for it. The trail coming up the slope is obvious so you can easily find the opening.

A special note about this Ice Cave—it's dangerous. People going in there have slipped on the ice and broken legs. You go in a ways on some ice that slopes down gradually towards the back of the cave. The entry is somewhat covered with dirt and sand from people coming in but to go very far you should have crampons and ropes and know how to use them. You soon reach a forty foot rappel down a frozen waterfall. From here you make another rappel and come to an area of beautiful ice crystals. Another longer rappel brings you near to the end. Huge icicles nearly a hundred feet tall and thirty feet around are found here. More interesting things may be seen in this cave but again this is only for the experienced caver with the right equipment.

If you're going on over to Fox Creek, you stay on the east side of the stream all the way. Back where the trail goes over to the creek to go to the Wind Cave, there is a sign showing the trail to Fox Creek. The canyon is open all the way to the end, with flowers covering the hillsides. Towering above are cliffs on both sides where caves and fossils may be found. The trail climbs gradually to the divide west of Fossil Mountain where it drops steeply down to Fox Creek. The Darby-Fox Creek loop hike would be a long one-day trip or a pleasant two-day hike. You could camp in the upper end on the Darby side on Fossil Mountain or there are some nice camping places shortly after you drop into Fox Creek Canyon.

There is a trail going up the North Fork of Darby Creek that leads up to the ridge overlooking Teton Canyon. It is difficult to find the beginning and the first mile or so of it. It takes off from the end of the road (more a route than a trail here) and you want to climb quite steeply so you'll cross over the North Fork about a mile up. You climb for about another half mile then it starts to contour and becomes a real good trail. This is not a maintained trail, has no signs and is little used. The reason it's there is because you can't go on up the canyon on the main creek because of all the cliffs that the stream drops over. This high route takes you around and above all this to the top of the canyon. It is a super rewarding trail as far as the view is concerned. There is a nice cirque under peak 10643 about a half mile above the trail and a spring about a mile from the end of the trail where the water runs year around. It is difficult to find water up there later in the summer.

At the end of the trail on the ridge about a mile northwest of Mount Meek, you have a fantastic view of Alaska Basin, the Tetons and the whole range. Mountain sheep use all this area around Mount Meek, Jedediah Smith and Bannon. There is a faint sheep trail leading around the base of these peaks to

Mountain Sheep, Jackson Hole News photo by Dan Abrams

another sheep camp high on the slops of Mount Bannon. This is a really beautiful area but it is difficult to get around because all of it is eroded limestone with very little soil, making walking precarious. Below Mount Bannon there is a huge glacial cirque with year around snow in it. Water is difficult to find but there are some large springs that come up, flow a ways then go back underground. This is a very good place to observe mountain sheep as there is a large herd that frequents this area.

SOUTH TETON CANYON TRAIL

USGS Maps: Granite Basin, Mount Bannon, Grand Teton.
Distances: Devils Stairs 2.7 miles, E.R. 3.7 miles.
              Teton Bench 4.7 miles, E.R. 7.9 miles.
              Alaska Basin 7.7 miles, E.R. 14.7 miles.

This is the main trail into Alaska Basin and is the main east-west route to either Death Canyon or Avalanche Canyon. It is one of the main routes used to go straight over the top wall of the Tetons and across to the east side. This canyon is quite heavily used by hikers but not nearly as much as is Garnet Canyon on the east side. It is probably the most used of the western trails because it has the best access road. No motorized vehicles are allowed on this trail and no open fires are permitted in Alaska Basin. Alaska Basin is a scenic but overly used camping area.

The access road starts at the bank corner in Driggs and goes east following the route through Alta towards the Targhee Ski Resort. You drive up Teton Canyon, going past the side road leading to the left to Targhee Ski Area. About five miles on up the canyon the road ends at Teton Campground. This is layed out in a circular pattern with picnic tables, trash cans, toilets, and is well maintained by the Forest Service. The trailhead is well marked and signed and is located at the transfer station at the end of the road past the campground. There is a parking area there for hikers and backpackers going in for several days.

The hiking is easy most of the way and follows the stream into Alaska Basin. After about three miles you reach a trail junction where to the right the trail goes up Devil's Stair onto the Teton Bench (see Devil's Stair Trail for this description). About a mile farther you begin a rather steep climb then level off and climb again until you join the Teton Crest Trail near a spring about a quarter of a mile from Basin Lakes in Alaska Basin.

Hurricane Pass is 2.6 miles to the north past Sunset Lake (camping area) along the Teton Crest Trail.

Mount Meek Pass is 2.4 miles to the southwest along the Teton Crest Trail. After climbing the Sheep Steps you will be on the Teton Bench and reach the side trail going northwest along the bench and back down Devil's Stair into Teton Canyon. The Teton Crest Trail goes on over Mount Meek Pass onto Death Canyon Shelf and on to Fox Creek Pass. (For more about this see Death Canyon Trail.)

Buck Mountain Pass is 2.6 miles to the southeast along the Alaska Basin Trail coming up out of Death Canyon.

Teton Canyon—Fox Creek Loop

A nice loop hike used by many people is to come up the South Fork of Teton Creek to Alaska Basin, cross the Death Canyon Shelf to Fox Creek Pass, and go down Fox Creek. This would be an easy three day backpacking trip. Some go the reverse way but probably the Teton Canyon first would be a little easier to get up. It would be eight miles to Alaska Basin, about four or so across Death Canyon Shelf, and seven or eight going down Fox Creek.

Devil's Stair—Teton Bench

About three miles up Teton Canyon you come to a signed, obvious fork in the trail. The Devil's Stairs Trail takes off to the right and climbs up onto a long bench above the canyon. It is a well used trail. Right at the start it is real steep, with numerous switchbacks and is not safe for horses. Hikers will have no problem with it.

The main attraction for this trail is the view all along the bench. There is an interesting lake up there and early in the season, waterfalls come off the cliffs. Also mountain sheep may be seen. This area is known as the Teton Bench and is much the same as the Death Canyon Shelf around the corner of Mount Meek to the south.

Another attraction of the bench are the vertical caves. Along this limestone formation deep caves and sink holes may be explored.

All along the bench there are beautiful campsites with spectacular views of Alaska Basin and the Tetons. There is plenty of water from springs or streams.

NORTH TETON CANYON TRAIL

USGS Maps: Granite Basin, Mount Moran, Grand Teton
Distances: Table Mountain 4.5 miles, E.R. 12.8 miles.

This trail leads up onto Table Mountain which is one of the best points on the range from which to view the spectacular peaks of the Tetons. It is heavily used, maintained, and is easy hiking although some sections are steep and rock scrambling is necessary to get on top.

The trail starts across the road to the north from Teton Campground. (To reach the campground, see South Teton Canyon Trail description.) You start switching upwards, following the North Fork and reach a trail junction in about a mile and a half. The trail taking off to the left goes up behind Freds Mountain over to South Leigh Creek. (More on this trail near the end of this chapter.)

Continuing on up the North Fork you climb gradually, staying on the north side above the stream. After about a mile, an interesting side trip may be made into an upper basin. After passing the trail branch leading over to South Leigh Creek, you make four creek crossings. Right at the fourth crossing, you've left the main stream and are starting up a side stream on the way to Table Mountain. At that point look back, due east of the trail and you'll see the main stream coming down some falls. You go over through that area and you'll see where someone has marked the trail with paint on the trees and rocks. You must go due east from the fourth creek crossing to get on it. It leads up through into a very large basin at the head of North

Teton Canyon. It is very isolated and rarely visited, with beautiful meadows and several lakes.

Going on up the trail you cross the stream a few times and enter the huge cirque below Table Mountain, which is southeast of you here. The trail swings to the west and you have some steep climbing to get above the headwall onto the ridge leading towards the top. There is a patch of snow on the north side of this ridge and in the early spring the snow extends over part of the trail, making an ice axe a necessity.

The trail disappears as you near the summit and you make your own way up the talus slope to the top. The view from the summit has no equal on the range. It was here that William Jackson took the first photographs of the Tetons. (More on this in High Adventure Trail description.)

Hurricane Pass may be reached from here by going down the ridge south of Table Mountain and skirting around peak 10635 to the west, staying as high as possible, and regaining the ridge south of the peak and continuing on south to Hurricane Pass. At the pass you join the Teton Crest Trail which goes south into Alaska Basin, or you can go east into the head of Cascade Canyon. From there you can cross over into either Garnet or Avalanche Canyons from the pass above Kit Lake.

North Fork—South Leigh Creek Side Trail

The trail going over to South Leigh Creek from North Teton Creek is maintained but steep and not a lot of people use it. There is a sign at the fork on North Teton a little over a mile from Teton Campground. The trail climbs steeply about two miles to the divide where there is a sign. From here you can turn left on a trail going down to the Grand Targhee Ski Resort. You can turn right across the divide and follow the contours around the mountain to South Leigh Lakes. Going straight ahead down the other side you'll cross a big flat area known as Beards Wheat Field. Freds Mountain is on your left to the west where some people do some climbing on the cliffs. This is in back of the ski area. The trail continues on down to join the South Leigh Creek Trail.

Grand Teton from No. Teton Canyon, Teton Trails
Photography.

FREDS MOUNTAIN TRAIL

USGS Map: Granite Basin
Distances: North Teton—South Leigh Trail 3.5 miles, E.R. 6.3
miles.
South Leigh Lakes 5 miles, E.R. 7.8 miles.

This trail runs from near the Grand Targhee Ski Resort up
around Freds Mountain to join the trail between North Teton
and South Leigh Creeks. It is an access trail to South Leigh
Lakes, starting almost a thousand feet higher than either Teton
Canyon or South Leigh Canyon.

The trail begins about a quarter of a mile before you reach
the Grand Targhee Ski Resort, which is located on a paved side
road off Teton Canyon. The canyon road starts at the bank
corner in the center of Driggs, Idaho. About a quarter of a mile
back (southwest) from the resort, a dirt side road takes off to

the east. There is no sign. It leads to Cold Springs where the trail starts.

It is a well beaten horse trail at the beginning which follows up Mill Creek about two miles of faintly steep climbing. Then towards the top it climbs steeply out of the basin, around Mary's Nipple and traverses above the cliffs to join the trail between North Teton and South Leigh Creeks.

There is no trail going over to South Leigh Lakes but it is easy to get there. From the trail junction you cross the divide to the north and then take off to the east contouring around the mountain on the same level and you'll reach the lakes in about a mile and a half of easy hiking. The lakes lie on a huge bench with cliffs all across under them. They are large beautiful lakes with plenty of good places to camp.

SOUTH LEIGH CREEK TRAIL

USGS Maps: Clawson, Granite Basin
Distances: Granite Basin 6.7 miles, E.R. 11.5 miles.
          South Leigh Lakes 7 miles, E.R. 11.8 miles.

This canyon is little used and the trail is easily followed, with little climbing for over half the way.

The main attraction up South Leigh Creek is to get into Granite Basin. It is a big wide beautiful canyon all the way, with flower covered bottom and good fishing and camping. There a lot of deer and bear up there also.

The road going up South Leigh Creek starts near Clawson, Idaho. You drive north from Clawson, cross South Leigh Creek and turn right (east) at the next corner where there are signs. You follow this dirt road where in about 2½ miles the road to North Leigh turns off to the left. Continue to the east on up South Leigh. There's a sign at the forest boundary. The road is good till you reach this boundary, then it gets rough and passable with slow care. There has been some timber cutting along this road which contributes to its roughness. There are deep ruts in places that you'll have to watch for.

The trail starts near the end of the road and across the stream (no bridge). The Beaver Creek Trail starts at the end of the road and goes up Beaver Creek and over the top to North Leigh. It is seldom used and not maintained.

There is plenty of room to park your car near the end of the road.

There is kind of a road that goes across the stream and the main trail goes this way. This old road goes on up South Leigh quite a ways. The trail is real gradual up a flat bottom canyon following the meadows where there is good fishing in the stream and the beaver ponds.

About three miles up the canyon a side trail comes in from the south which goes over to the North Fork of Teton Creek. This trail is pretty steep for about a mile and a half and then levels off pretty much. This is an access route to South Leigh Lakes and for details and an easier route see the trail description for Freds Mountain Trail.

Most people go on up South Leigh Creek where in about a mile the trail turns up Granite Creek where in about two more miles (with some steep climbing the first mile) you'll reach Granite Basin. This basin is one of the prettiest areas on this side of the divide. It is a very scenic cirque sitting under peaks and cliffs all around. The huge lakes have good fishing. The upper lake has small fish but down in the lower lakes there are three pound cutthroats.

The trail going up Andy Stone Creek is a real old one in very poor condition. It is seldom used and advised against.

From the upper Granite Basin Lake, the trail continues to the north, up and over to join the Teton Crest Trail and the South Fork of North Leigh Creek Trail coming up from Green Lakes.

NORTH FORK LEIGH CREEK

USGS Maps: Clawson, Granite Basin
Distances:
Via Green Mountain Trail: Green Lakes 4 miles, E.R. 8.6 miles.
        Junction with Teton Crest Trail 5.2 miles, E.R. 11.2
        miles.
        Granite Basin 6.7 miles, E.R. 13.7 miles.
Via South Fork North Leigh Trail: Join South Leigh Trail 4.5
        miles, E.R. 8.9 miles.
        Granite Basin 6.1 miles, E.R. 12.3 miles.

Two main trails lead out of this canyon: the Green Mountain Trail, an easy hike into the beautiful Green Lakes area; and South Fork of North Leigh Trail, an excellent route into Granite Basin. The North Fork Leigh Creek Trail is an old dead-end trail, not maintained and seldom used.

The road leading up North Leigh Creek Canyon starts near Clawson, Idaho. You drive north from Clawson to the next corner, where there are signs, and turn right. You follow this good dirt road for about 2½ miles and turn left over a cattle guard onto another signed dirt road. This has been a fairly rough road but it was reworked in the summer of 1975 and should be fairly passable for a sedan. You drive to the end of the road and cross an old bridge where you will see an old saw mill over to the right. Follow the blazed logging road straight ahead to where the trail forks. The left (north) fork is the Green Mountain Trail. The right (south) fork is the South Fork of North Leigh Trail (shown on USGS maps as Andy Stone Trail).

Green Mountain Trail

From the trail fork you proceed up the slope staying north of and above Tin Cup Creek. The Green Mountain Trail has been used as a road but it is now closed off. It climbs steeply for about two miles, follows the ridge a short ways then drops over the other side. Here you traverse pretty much on the level for about a mile around Green Mountain and reach the largest of the lakes. These lakes are very pretty and in a scenic location so they get fairly heavy use. There are many good campsites and pretty good fishing here.

Just before reaching the first large lake, the trail forks. The right fork stays above the lake and goes on over to Granite Basin, about two miles away. The other fork goes down to the lake, crosses to other lakes, then continues on to join the Teton Crest Trail, running from Granite Basin north below the divide to South Badger Creek and on over Dead Horse Pass.

South Fork of North Leigh Trail

This trail was cleared of fallen trees in the fall of 1975 so is in pretty good shape.

At the trail fork described earlier, this trail takes off to the right (south) and climbs gradually all the way. It is an easier route to Granite Basin as it has no real steep places like you have coming up Granite Creek out of South Leigh Canyon.

Another point of interest on this trail is the presence of fossils near the upper part of the trail on Bear Mountain. These may be found along the south side of the mountain, about a quarter mile west after crossing the highest point on the trail.

When the trail starts down, it swings off to the east and joins the South Leigh Creek Trail, about a mile and a half from the upper Granite Basin Lake.

Nature cannot be surprised in undress.
Beauty breaks in everywhere.

—Ralph Waldo Emerson

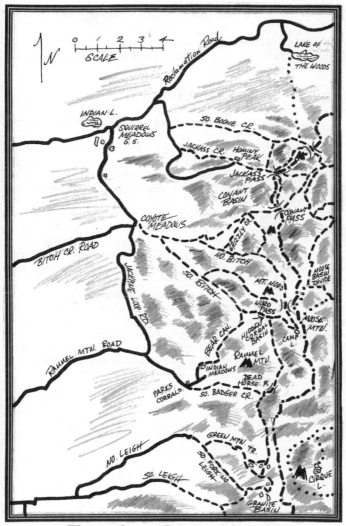

Targhee Side, North

SOUTH BADGER CREEK TRAIL

USGS Maps: McReynolds Reservoir, Rammel Mountain
Distances: Junction with Teton Crest Trail 4.1 miles, E.R. 5.6
      miles.

The main attraction of this trail is the good fishing and
camping places along a very pretty South Badger Creek. It also
is an access to the Teton Crest Trail that crosses the upper end
of the basin. It is well maintained.

The trail head is signed and is in the Parks Corral area on
Rammel Mountain Road. Best access to this road is along the
Jackpine Loop Road coming from Coyote Meadows on Bitch
Creek (see Bitch Creek Trail Description). You can park your
car near the trailhead.

The trail leaves the road at about 8100 feet elevation and
drops off to the south where in about a mile it reaches South
Badger Creek. For about two miles the trail hardly climbs at all
as it follows the stream through lush meadows where generally
there are sheep grazing. Fishing is good both upstream and
down from where the trail joins it.

Further up the basin, the trail starts climbing and in about a
mile joins the Teton Crest Trail going north and south. It's real
steep whichever way you go. Turning south, it's about seven
miles to Granite Basin. Turning north you climb to Dead Horse
Pass and cross over into Bitch Creek. Climbing to the pass, the
route is marked only by rock cairns and is not a well defined
trail.

Targhee Cutthroat Trout, Bridger-Teton National Forest
photo by D. A. Colwell.

SOUTH BITCH CREEK TRAIL

USGS Maps: McReynolds Reservoir, Rammel Mountain,
           Ranger Peak
Distances: Hidden Corral Basin 8.5 miles, E.R. 10.5 miles.
          Camp Lake 10.5 miles, E.R. 15.5 miles.
          Dead Horse Pass 12.8 miles, E.R. 17 miles.
          Nord Pass via Carrot Ridge 9.8 miles, E.R. 15.6
          miles.

This trail is mainly used by fishermen wanting to get into the
lush meadows that line the stream for many miles, all the way
to Hidden Corral Basin and beyond. Camp Lake, which is on a
side stream above Hidden Corral Basin is also a popular fishing
and backpacking spot. This trail provides a main access to other
trails serving scenic areas north and south, and also to Moose
Basin in Teton National Park. Horse outfits use this trail a lot,
too.

Trail begins at Coyote Meadows. To get there start at Lamont which is 18 miles on highway 32 from Ashton, or 23 miles from Driggs on highways 33 and 32. From Lamont, go north one mile and turn right (east). From there it's three miles of gravelled road and nine miles of dirt road to Coyote Meadows. Four wheel drive vehicles recommended for the dirt road. A new gravel road is planned for Coyote Meadows in 1976 or 1977 which should provide good access. There is parking space for fifteen vehicles at the meadows.

The trail is a good one and has a sign at the trailhead. It climbs gradually up to a low saddle, crosses over and traverses to cross Crater Creek, then again climbs to another low saddle where the trail splits. The North Bitch Creek Trail takes off to the left and the South Bitch Creek Trail goes to the right.

The trail follows along the edge of the meadows along the stream all the way to Bitch Creek Narrows. It's about eight miles to the narrows, and one can pull back into the trees and camp anywhere along the way.

Bitch Creek Narrows is an interesting narrow slot through the canyon. The story goes that in the early days horse rustlers came up here to hide their horses. They could lay a few poles across the narrows and keep them in the basin.

Some rock climbing can be done at the narrows but this is not really the local hot spot for climbers.

Bear Canyon Trail

About a mile before reaching the narrows, a trail takes off to the right (south) and goes up Bear Canyon. The trail is well named as it's a bear to get through. It is very steep at the Bear Canyon end and passes through two big boggy areas and a lot of downed timber. It is not maintained and the fallen trees across the trail haven't been cut for quite a few years. Some people like to use it starting from Indian Meadows as it's a closer access to Bitch Creek from Tetonia. It is a rough trail and not recommended.

Less than a mile past the narrows you reach Hidden Corral Basin. This is a huge flower-covered basin with a deep crystal clear stream flowing through it, containing large cutthroat trout. All the way upstream from here is good fishing in the stream and beaver ponds. A sign at the trial junction designates Camp Lake Trail climbing up out of the basin to the east.

Going on up Bitch Creek it is a very pretty hike the remaining four miles or so to Dead Horse Pass. The trail gradually climbs up along the stream for about three miles then climbs steeply to the pass. There are some really beautiful places along this section of small streams in heavily wooded areas.

From the upper end of the canyon there are two routes to take up to Dead Horse Pass. The main trail leaves Bitch Creek, taking off to the right and goes steeply up to the pass. The other route follows on up Bitch Creek to its upper reaches then goes on up the ridge south of the pass, then descends to join the main trail at the pass. The latter is a longer, more gradual route.

The trail from the pass descends very steeply into South Badger Creek, then goes up again and over into Granite Basin.

Camp Lake Trail

From Hidden Corral Basin on South Bitch Creek the trail climbs steeply most of the two miles to Camp Lake. From there it climbs a little, then traverses north across Moose Mountain Slide area to Nord Pass. From the pass you can cross the divide, going on either side of Moose Mountain, into Moose Basin in the park.

Silver Creek—Moose Mountain Route

This route uses parts of three trails to get from South Bitch Creek to Moose Mountain where you can cross the divide into Moose Basin and go down Webb Canyon or Owl Creek.

It starts about four miles from Coyote Meadows on the South Bitch Creek Trail. It takes off to the left about a mile after crossing Silver Creek. This is the south end of the Conant Basin Trail and you follow it to the top of the ridge separating South Bitch from North Bitch. Here you reach a trail fork and take the Carrot Ridge Trail to the right up to the top of the ridge. From here you'll follow the Mt. Nord Trail around Mt. Nord and over to Nord Pass. From the pass you can go around either side of Moose Mountain, cross the divide and drop into Moose Basin.

NORTH BITCH CREEK TRAIL

USGS Maps: McReynolds Reservoir, Rammel Mountain, Granite Peak, Grassy Lake Reservoir
Distances: Nord Pass 10.5 miles, E.R. 16.5 miles.
Conant Pass 6.5 miles, E.R. 11.3 miles.

This trail is in fair condition with heavy downfall and intermittent maintenance. It provides access to Grizzly Creek and Berry Creek across the divide by way of Conant Pass, and Moose Basin, also on the Teton Park side via Nord Pass. North Bitch Creek has about the same volume of water as South Bitch but the canyon is much more narrow. As a result, there are fewer meadows and the stream is not heavily used for fishing. This trail is also used to reach Camp Lake, about two miles beyond Nord Pass above the end of the stream.

This trail starts on the South Bitch Creek Trail about a mile from its beginning at Coyote Meadows. To reach Coyote Meadows, see the description for South Bitch Creek Trail.

The North Bitch Creek Trail stays high above the creek for about 2½ miles, then the Conant Pass Trail takes off to the left and climbs to Conant Pass. The North Bitch Creek Trail descends to Bitch Creek and follows it to Grizzly Creek where the Conant Basin Trail takes off to the left and goes up above Grizzly Creek, crosses the Conant Pass Trail and goes on north to join the Jackass (Hominy Creek) Trail southwest of Hominy Peak.

After crossing Grizzly Creek, the North Bitch Trail climbs above North Bitch Creek, passing south of peak 7,859, and continues to climb for about a half mile where it joins the Teton Crest Trail. This continues on fairly level for a ways, then begins to descend to the stream. Near the stream, the Carrot Ridge Trail takes off to the southwest. Our trail again climbs to the east and skirts the basin above the stream for about two miles of gradual climbing to reach Nord Pass.

At Nord Pass you are about two miles from Camp Lake to the south. Also from the pass it is easy to cross the divide to the east into Moose Basin. Going across north of Moose Mountain, you can hike north along the upper part of Moose Basin and reach the Webb Canyon Trail south of Moose Basin Divide.

HOMINY CREEK (JACKASS TRAIL)

USGS Map: Grassy Lake Reservoir
Distances: Hominy Peak 4 miles, E.R. 7.4 miles.
             Jackass Pass 6 miles, E.R. 9.8 miles.

   This trail provides access to the high country at the north end
of the Teton Range. It ties in with the Teton Crest Trail at
Jackass Pass where another trail crosses into the park going
down to Berry Creek. It receives light maintenance, with the
downfall cleared. It has a more gradual grade than South Boone
and follows the ridge tops most of the way, providing a better
view of the surrounding country. There is also a jeep road to
Hominy Peak on another route but it will probably be closed in
the near future.
   To reach the trailhead follow the directions given for South
Boone Trail. Continue further on the Jackass Road (poor dirt
road) another mile and a half to the trailhead where there is a
sign reading "Hominy Trail, Hominy Butte 4". There is room to
park about fifteen cars here.
   The trail takes off gradually up the mountain, staying mostly
on the ridges above Jackass Creek. On the peak there used to
be a Forest Service fire lookout station.
   From the peak, the trail continues east fairly level and in
about a mile and a half a side trail comes in on the left (north)
from South Boone Creek. Continuing on, you will reach Jackass
Pass and join the Teton Crest Trail in less than a half mile of
gradual climbing. The Teton Crest Trail goes north around
Survey Peak to join South Boone Trail. Going south, it crosses
to Conant Pass and goes on to Nord Pass and South Bitch
Creek. Also from Jackass Pass, you can go into the park down
to Berry Creek.

SOUTH BOONE CREEK TRAIL

USGS Map: Grassy Lake Reservoir
Distances: Survey Peak, join Teton Crest Trail 8 miles, E.R. 12
miles.

This trail provides access to the high country at the north end
of the Teton Range. It ties in with a trail going into the park via
Berry Creek and joins the Teton Crest Trail going south to
Grizzly Creek and Bitch Creek. It receives light maintenance
and has a moderate grade with a mile of steep hiking at the
head of the canyon. It is also used by sheep for range accesss.

To reach the trailhead, you go on the Reclamation Road 25
miles of gravelled road east from Ashton, Idaho, or 21 miles of
dirt road from Flagg Ranch, Wyoming. Near Gibson Meadows
you turn off southeast and go two miles on Jackass Road (a poor
dirt road) to the trailhead. The road from Ashton opens about
June 1. The road from Flagg Ranch opens about July 1. There is
a sign on the left side of Jackass Road at South Boone Creek
reading "South Boone Trail, Survey Peak 8". There is parking
space at the trailhead for about ten cars.

Hiking the trail is fairly easy as it climbs gradually along the
north side of the stream through timber country. Near the head
of the canyon where you start to climb and leave the stream, a
side trail takes off to the right and climbs about a mile and a half
to join the Jackass Trail (Hominy Creek Trail) going on to
Jackass Pass. Continuing on up Boone Creek Trail you soon get
above Timberline where you must pay close attention or else
you'll loose the faint trail. It continues around north of Survey
Peak and joins the Teton Crest Trail and the trail coming up
from Berry Creek near the divide.

The Teton Crest Trail climbs up and around the north side of
Survey Peak and reaches Jackass Pass in about two miles.
Then it continues on south fairly level to Conant Pass and
beyond above Grizzly and North Bitch Creeks.

A loop trail could be made by going west from Jackass Pass
less than half mile on the Jackass Trail and turn off to the right
(north) and cross back to rejoin the South Boone Trail which
will take you back to your car.

Teton High Country, Jackson Hole News photo by R. Murphy

High Adventure Trail

USGS Maps: Rendezvous Peak, Mount Bannon, Grand Teton,
Mount Moran, Granite Basin, Rammel Mountain,
Ranger Peak, Grassy Lake Reservoir

Distances: Phillips Pass 4 miles, E.R. 6.3 miles.
Marion Lake 11 miles, E.R. 16.8 miles.
Fox Creek Pass 13 miles, E.R. 19.4 miles.
Alaska Basin 18.5 miles, E.R. 25.5 miles.
Hurricane Pass 21.5 miles, E.R. 30.2 miles.
No. Teton-So. Leigh Jct. 27.5 miles, E.R. 36.8 miles.
Granite Basin 36 miles, E.R. 53.1 miles.
Badger Creek 42.5 miles, E.R. 60.8 miles.
Hidden Corral Basin 48 miles, E.R. 69.7 miles.
Nord Pass 51.5 miles, E.R. 77.1 miles.
Conant Pass 58 miles, E.R. 87.2 miles.
Jackass Pass 60 miles, E.R. 89.7 miles.
So. Boon Tr. 62.5 miles, E.R. 92.9 miles.
Lake of the Woods 67.5 miles, E.R. 97.9 miles.

The High Adventure Trail is the name that I have given to a combination of trails which run along the west side of the Teton Range all the way from Phelps Canyon on the south to Lake of the Woods on the north. As we go northward, I will point out the various other trails that intersect this High Adventure Trail from both the Idaho side and the Teton Park side. This will set up a labyrinth of trails which are accessible to the backpacker but little known and little used. This will make the entire west side of the Tetons available to almost any backpacker who wants to take a longer trip in an isolated and beautiful country.

This system of trails and connecting trails goes all the way from the Teton Pass Road near the famous Glory Snow Slide area all the way north to the Grassy Lake area, where one meets the road running crosswise from the Flagg Ranch to Ashton, Idaho. This road is sometimes called the Reclamation Road. The distance from the Grassy Lake Road to the Teton Pass Road is approximately 40 miles as the crow flies. Of course, the way the trail runs through the crests of the Teton Range on this particular trail, which is nearly always on the Idaho side, represents quite a few more miles. One of the interesting parts of this trail is that except for approximately three miles near Marion Lake and for a distance of about four miles on the Death Canyon Shelf, all the rest of these trails are outside of the Grand Teton National Park. Except for those two small traverses in the park, no permission would be necessary from the Grand Teton National Park to traverse this area, and then only if one wished to camp in the park.

This is a varied country of beautiful timber and scenic alpine meadows, where you will see snow fields, lakes, rivers, beautiful views, and which represents a high altitude trail, much of the time in the vicinity of the timberline or above.

Although along this trail there are many ups and downs, the traversing of this entire trail would be practical on a backpacking trip of approximately ten days to two weeks. Several spots along the way, there will be some fishing.

PHILLIPS PASS TRAIL

The southern end of our High Adventure Trail starts up the Phillips Pass Trail from an elevation of approximately 7800 feet on the Teton Pass Road approximately a mile below the large snow slide area that goes on the southeast side of Mt. Glory. The road coming up from Jackson Hole makes a large bend here and goes straight north for about a mile where it makes a sharp turn towards the west and then turns southwest. Just shortly after this last turn towards the southwest, you will cross an old logging road which takes off towards the north about a quarter of a mile past where the main road crosses the north fork of Trail Creek. This old road goes up towards Phillips Ridge. (See Phillips Pass Trail description elsewhere for detailed description of this beginning.) About a quarter of a mile up this road, our trail takes off towards the north and goes up in elevation a couple of hundred feet before crossing over into the head waters of Phillips Canyon. Where this trail crosses the stream first in upper Phillips Canyon, another trail takes off to the left climbing up to Ski Lake about a mile above, but our trail continues in a northerly direction climbing gradually for another half mile and crosses the small stream which runs out of Ski Lake. From there on the trail keeps going straight north, climbing gradually and traversing the mountain until it crosses the Middle Fork of Phillips Creek and there it turns northwest again and rises rapidly above timberline to Phillips Pass at an elevation of 8,932 feet.

At Phillips Pass, another trail comes up from the Coal Creek Camp Ground at 7,300 feet elevation on the Idaho side of Teton Pass. One could also start from that campground, come up to Phillips Pass, and join our High Adventure Trail there. One would start from approximately 500 feet lower elevation. So, the trail coming from the Coal Creek campground would be perhaps a mile longer in length and would necessitate a climb of an extra 500 feet in elevation.

TETON CREST TRAIL

This section of our High Adventure Trail is known as the Teton Crest Trail and runs from Phillips Pass on the south to Hurricane Pass north of Alaska Basin, which is at an elevation of around 10,400 feet.

From Phillips Pass the trail continues almost directly due east and follows the divide going up the ridge approaching the top of Rendezvous Mountain for about two miles where it reaches its highest elevation in this area of about 9,800 feet. This ridge is the divide separating the drainage between Jackson's Hole on the east and Pierre's Hole or Teton Basin on the west. The trail continues dropping steeply for a ways and then follows the contours of the mountain for about three miles where you reach a junction of the trail coming up from Moose Creek and Moose Meadows, joining our High Adventure Trail at about the 8,800 foot elevation. Near here, another trail takes off to the west and climbs up to Moose Lake about a mile and a half away and about 400 feet higher in elevation.

Our trail continues to the north switchbacking steeply up to a divide where at about 9,000 feet in elevation you will cross over into the Teton Park in the upper reaches of Granite Canyon.

Going through the divide, one will traverse for about three quarters of a mile where one will hit the junction of another trail coming up from Granite Creek in Granite Canyon. This fork is called the Middle Fork Cutoff Trail and goes down for about two and a half miles to join the Granite Creek Trail near the patrol cabin where the north fork and the middle fork of Granite Creek come together.

The Game Creek Trail takes off from the Teton Crest Trail up on the ridge between the middle and North Forks of Granite Creek. It's difficult to find and it has no sign. There are rock cairns marking the way and once you're on it, it's easy to follow. You follow up the ridge mentioned above and it goes along a bench and through some steep places up onto another bench. Then it climbs up to the forest divide through some scree. The trail switchbacks and is covered with snow until late in the season. It's quite spectacular as you climb up this area as it looks like you're going right up to the sky. When you reach the divide, the trail drops steeply down the other side into the Game Creek drainage.

Continuing on our High Adventure Trail, we proceed northward through the upper reaches of Granite Canyon maintaining an altitude of around 9,000 feet but going up and down a hundred feet or so now and then until you reach Marion Lake which sets below Housetop Mountain at about 9,300 feet in elevation. About a half a mile before reaching Marion Lake another trail joins from the right which comes up the North Fork of Granite Creek. A patrol cabin is located about two and a half miles down from the Teton Crest Trail. Also, the Open Canyon Trail joins the North Fork Trail coming up about a mile above the patrol cabin.

At Marion Lake you are approximately seven miles from Phillips Pass. The trail skirts around the east side of Marion Lake crossing the stream at its lower outlet. After leaving Marion Lake, you will climb fairly steeply for a quarter of a mile and reach a pass along the divide separating the Teton side from the Targhee at an elevation of about 9,600 feet. The trail follows the divide for maybe a quarter of a mile and then leaves the Teton boundaries to traverse almost directly north for about a mile and a half around the base of Spearhead Peak where you will reach Fox Creek Pass at nearly the same elevation of 9,600 feet. Here a trail joins which came up from Fox Creek on the Idaho side to the west. Our trail goes north for approximately a quarter of a mile to where the Death Canyon Trail joins it, coming up from the right.

Our trail continues towards the north and a little bit east on to the beautiful Death Canyon Shelf for approximately three and a half miles without gaining any significant elevation. This trail is almost level with a very precipitous canyon wall above and below and represents one of the most beautiful stretches of trail to be found anywhere.

After the three and a half mile hike along the Death Canyon Shelf, one will reach the Mt. Meek Pass at about 9,700 feet in elevation which is on the divide where one will again leave the Teton Park and enter the Idaho drainage.

We then continue in a northeasterly direction for about a quarter of a mile below the pass where a trail comes in from the left going off towards the northwest. That trail follows gradually down a stream on a wide shelf for about four miles before descending the Devil's Stairs and joining the Alaska Basin Trail which comes up the south fork of Teton Creek from the Teton Campground below.

Reflections, Jackson Hole News photo by R. Murphy

Continuing along our High Adventure Trail for about a half a mile beyond the junction with the Teton Canyon Trail, one comes to what is known as the Sheep Steps where one zig zags down a very steep slope for a short distance. The old trails at the head of Death Canyon were made by the sheep herders in the early days. The first settlements in Teton Basin, or Pierre's Hole as I used to know it, and the area at the head of Death Canyon were great country for herding sheep in the summer time. These herds at times came into the upper reaches of Death Canyon where there is very good pasture in open country and scattered timber. There was some conflict in the early days between the sheep herders who came down into Death Canyon and the cattle people from Jackson Hole. Sheep were never allowed in Jackson Hole due to the pressure of the cattlemen who had the political control of the valley. The last trip that I made through this country, sheep were still grazing in this region around the upper end of Death Canyon. However, since part of this is now in the national park, I doubt if the sheep are allowed to graze on this side of the divide.

After our trail gets down the Sheep Steps, the trail turns suddenly directly towards the east for approximately a half a mile and then, crossing the south fork of Teton Creek, it turns northeast again along the beautiful Basin Lakes and here we are in the upper regions of Alaska Basin.

As far as I can remember, this area was first called Alaska Basin by myself or by Mr. Owen when we brought horses up Death Canyon and camped in here in 1924 before climbing the Grand Teton, starting from the west side of the mountain.

Near the Basin Lakes, one will hit the Alaska Basin Trail that is a recently man-made trail that goes over towards Buck Mountain and Static Peak and on down to join the Death Canyon Trail at a patrol cabin at an elevation of approximately 8,000 feet. Also, this Alaska Basin Trail from near Basin Lakes in Alaska Basin goes down the south fork of Teton Creek to the Teton Campground far below.

Our High Adventure Trail proceeds from the Basin Lakes northward for about a mile to the beautiful Sunset Lake which is almost due west of the South Teton Peak. If one camps in this vicinity, it is well worth the effort to hike towards the east for about a mile to the very perpendicular wall and look down at Avalanche Canyon (and Snow Drift Lake in its upper reaches below you) and about a mile to the southeast and straight down into Taggart Lake 4,000 feet below. Also, from this point on the wall, one can make his way down into the saddle and cross on an easy traverse towards the northwest to Ice Flow Lake which sets below the west wall of the Middle Teton Peak. It is also possible from this saddle below the wall above Sunset Lake to proceed almost directly east and climb the ridge up to South Teton Peak. Or, one can traverse around towards the north along the west side of South Teton and enter the south branch of Garnet Canyon and descend Garnet Canyon to Bradley and Taggart Lakes or Lupine Meadows near Jenny Lake.

From Sunset Lake the trail continues north for approximately two miles to Hurricane Pass where you cross to the other side of the divide above the Schoolroom Glacier and Schoolroom Lake below it. From here the trail continues down into the south fork of Cascade Canyon where that trail continues on out to Jenny Lake.

Schoolroom Glacier, Jackson Hole News photo by Cammie Pyle

HIGH ADVENTURE TRAIL FROM HURRICANE PASS NORTH

Our High Adventure Trail stays on the Idaho side at Hurricane Pass and continues to the north below the divide. There is no maintained trail for about two miles, however, the route follows just below the divide and swings off to the left and joins the Table Mountain Trail on the west side of that mountain. One would be advised not to lose or gain too much altitude, but to traverse at much the same level from the west side of the pass towards Table Mountain, which is in a straight line about a mile and a half due north from Hurricane Pass.

Table Mountain presents what many people think is the most spectacular mountain view in North America. It was on the top of Table Mountain that the first pictures of the Tetons were taken in 1872 when William Jackson, the pioneer photographer with the Hayden Expedition, brought mules to the top of Table Mountain from Pierre's Hole and set up his dark room in a tent. There he prepared his glass plates on the spot and took some pictures of the Grand Tetons and the other Teton Peaks which today are still considered great photographs. He continued from Table Mountain on into Yellowstone Park where he took the first photographs which authenticated the wild tales of Jim Bridger and other early explorers. These pictures were perhaps more influential than any other thing in causing the Congress of the United States to establish the Yellowstone Area as a National Park. It was also his influence and photographs that helped to establish the U.S. Geological Survey and to take the administration of the West from under the control of the Army and put it into the hands of the Department of the Interior.

About a quarter of a mile to the west and a little bit south from the top of Table Mountain and approximately 500 feet lower, one will hit an old trail going to the west and a little bit north down the northwest ridge of Table Mountain. From there at an elevation of approximately 10,400 feet on the Table Mountain Trail, the trail leads down on the North Fork of Teton Creek. There, the trail follows generally along the north side of the creek down for approximately two miles to the junction of the North Fork Teton Trail and the trail going over to South

Leigh Creek at an elevation of about 7,800 feet. This will be a total drop of approximately 2,200 feet if one does not go to the top of Table Mountain.

When one reaches the fork of the trail at 7,800 feet, one will take the right hand trail and here again gain elevation quite rapidly while going approximately ¾ of a mile west on the trail and then turning and going approximately a mile north where one comes to a saddle going over the divide into the South Leigh Creek Drainage at an elevation of approximately 9,600 feet. Just before one gets over the pass, one comes to a junction of the trail that runs directly west for about three miles to the headquarters of the Grand Targhee Ski Resort where there is a paved road leading out to Driggs, idaho. The views and the country at the Pass are extremely beautiful. From the Pass going north about 2½ miles, one comes to another junction in the trail where you join the South Leigh Creek Trail which comes up South Leigh Creek from the end of a dirt road about three miles down the stream.

Continuing along the High Adventure Trail, one turns to the right and goes up the south fork of Leigh Creek, crossing the creek at an elevation of approximately 7,200 feet. After going along through the flat timbered country for about a quarter of amile, the trail rises very, very steeply for approximately a mile to the junction of the South Fork of North Leigh Creek Trail at an elevation of 8,600 feet. From there the trail goes over into Granite Basin and the Granite Basin Lakes. This is a beautiful camping area. These lakes have fish in them and this would be a good place to camp for a few days just to camp and fish. To the east, one can climb up onto the divide where one can look down to Lake Solitude and Cascade Creek to the southeast and Leigh Canyon and Mt. Moran to the northeast. These represent some of the best views in the Tetons. This side trip to the divide is very rewarding.

From Granite Basin, the trail makes a circle back towards the north and then swings around towards the west to the junction of a trail that's called the Green Mountain Trail which goes past the Green Lakes. However, our trail continues north, going past the Upper Green Lakes where it will join another trail that also heads back down the mountain to the left and joins the

Green Mountain Trail. From this point, our trail heads north for approximately four miles, keeping near timberline and following along the divide with some excellent views. Another trail coming up from Badger Creek from the left soon joins our trail.

After crossing the upper part of South Badger Creek, our trail rises very, very steeply to Dead Horse Pass which is a pass between Badger Creek and Bitch Creek drainages to the north. This pass was called Dead Horse Pass because of the many horses lost going over this very, very rough trail by the sheepherders who were taking their sheep over to get to the pastures to the north. From the top of Dead Horse Pass, our trail continues down to the north and a little bit east to the south fork of Bitch Creek. The trail then goes down this creek approximately three miles to the Hidden Corral Basin. The trail travels along the north side of Bitch Creek for this three miles and there is excellent camping along here. As well as camping, there is some fishing and it's especially good around Hidden Corral Basin.

Mt. Moran from So. Badger Canyon, Teton Trails Photography

Our High Adventure Trail continues east and a little south from the Hidden Corral Basin on the Camp Lake Trail back up towards the divide for approximately two miles to Camp Lake. Here it again turns north and goes through the scattered timber country for about a mile and a half where it meets a trail coming up the north fork of Bitch Creek. (Continuing on up to the divide near Moose Mountain, one can easily walk over the divide and down into Moose Basin on Moose Creek in Webb Canyon.) From this junction one goes through what is known as Nord Pass about a quarter of a mile to the north and continues north and a little bit towards the west for about three and a half miles where one meets another junction on the North Bitch Creek Trail. From this junction one continues on north for approximately three miles where another trail comes in from Grizzly Creek which goes down and joins the North Bitch Creek Trail. At this junction, one turns sharply towards the east and goes approximately a mile and a half gaining altitude quite rapidly to Conant Pass.

At Conant Pass there is another trail junction where one trail goes over the divide and down Berry Creek to where it runs into Jackson Lake. The High Adventure Trail continues directly towards the north and for about two miles follows along near the divide, crossing it two or three times. You will soon reach Jackass Pass where a trail going to the left will go approximately two miles down to the old Hominy Peak Ranger Station. There, a dirt road comes up to the Ranger Station. Also at the pass, another trail goes directly to the east down to Berry Creek. From this pass one travels northeast around Survey Peak and meets another trail that comes up South Boone Creek. That trail goes to the right to a pass, crosses over, and goes down to Berry Creek.

The rest of the trip to the Lake of the Woods is an easy cross-country hike through rolling country where one should not meet any insurmountable obstacles en route. By going down the trail heading towards South Boone Creek for approximately a half to three quarters of a mile, and then leaving the trail, taking off directly to the north, you will be approximately four miles from the Lake of the Woods. This is timbered country all the way and there is no significant gain or loss in elevation. By following your compass due north, you should hit the lake in about three or four hours.

When one reaches the Lake of the Woods, one traverses around the lake to the west where one will find a Boy Scout Camp at the end of the lake. There is a new road coming in to the camp. That road goes northward for about two miles where it joins the main road that goes from the Flagg Ranch to Ashton, Idaho. From that road, one can go to the Flagg Ranch where you'll reach the paved road running from Jackson north to Yellowstone Park. Going to the west, one would reach the paved road near Ashton, Idaho.

Other Guide Books Available
from:

Wasatch Publishers, Inc.
4647 Idlewild Rd.
Salt Lake City, Utah 84117

WIND RIVER TRAILS by Finis Mitchell, $2.95, Pub. 1975. Paperback, 4½ by 7 inches, 144 pages, 30 photos, 12 maps. A backpacking and fishing guide giving information about the trails, fishing, wildlife, glaciers, peaks, 4,000 lakes, and 800 miles of streams in Wyoming's fabulous Wind River Range.

HIGH UINTA TRAILS by Mel Davis, $2.95, Pub. 1974 Paperback, 4½ by 7 inches, 132 pages, 7 maps. A hiking, backpacking, fishing and camping guide to the High Uinta Primitive and Wilderness Area in northeastern Utah. Contains detailed trail information, maps, lakes index, fishing information, and tips for the wilderness backpackers.

WASATCH TRAILS by Betty Bottcher and Mel Davis, $1.50, Pub. 1973. Paperback, 4½ by 7 inches, 77 pages, 5 maps. An illustrated hiking guide to an unsuspected world of mountain hiking within minutes of downtown Salt Lake City, Utah.

CACHE TRAILS by Mel Davis and Ann Schimpf, $1.50, Pub. in 1974. Paperback, 4½ by 7 inches, 96 pages, 5 maps. An illustrated hiking guide to three dozen mountain trails in the Cache Valley surrounding Logan, Utah.

The above books are available postpaid, dealer inquiries invited.